Richard S_____ ___vi
ing wom_____ D _____ h
and he d_____ M
of the women _ _ 2001   sc
their ongoing grief with ramin,   th
were telling him things they had nev_____ el
This inspired him to gather some of these stories in a bo
so that other women could benefit from their experienc

WHEN YOUR PARTNER DIES

Stories of women who have
lost their husbands

Richard Stanton

ALLEN & UNWIN

For Len

First published in 1999 by
Allen & Unwin
9 Atchison Street, St Leonards NSW 1590 Australia
Phone: (61 2) 8425 0100
Fax: (61 2) 9906 2218
E-mail: frontdesk@allen-unwin.com.au
Web: http://www.allen-unwin.com.au

National Library of Australia
Cataloguing-in-Publication entry:

Stanton, Richard, 1951–.
When your partner dies: stories of women
who have lost their husbands.

ISBN 1 86448 510 8.

1. Widowhood. 2. Bereavement. I. Title.

155.937

Set in 11/13 pt Garamond Book by DOCUPRO, Sydney
Printed and bound by Australian Print Group, Maryborough, Vic.

10 9 8 7 6 5 4 3 2 1

CONTENTS

ACKNOWLEDGMENTS

It is difficult to know where to begin acknowledging the women who have offered me unconditional support and inspiration for this work. For the most part, all my support has come from women.

Without the consent of the ten women whose profiles appear here, there would, of course, be no book. For their willingness to speak openly and freely about their individual plights I thank them unconditionally.

The book may not have seen the light of day if it were not for the considered comments of Dr Christine Everingham of Macquarie University's Sociology Department, who initially pointed me away from the prospects of a long dry sociological summer and towards the reality of commercialisation. Christine's ability to clearly enunciate my goals made the task of finding my first interviewee far easier than I had imagined.

Helen Yardley of the English Department at Macquarie University also deserves special thanks for her continued support of the project, for creating a 'snowball effect', for providing literary and journalistic comment on my overall approach to the work and, as my Master's supervisor, for her ability to connect the seemingly disparate paths of literature, public relations and politics.

To Helen Bassett I owe a debt of gratitude for being the 'guinea pig'—my first interviewee after being widowed for such a short time. Without her courage to continue in spite of an overwhelming volume of tears, I may have given up the ghost very early in the piece.

Others who deserve my thanks and gratitude for providing inspiration are Wendy Vines, Bron Reid and Sue Graham.

I also thank my publisher Elizabeth Weiss, firstly for assessing the work as a commercial possibility and also for her balanced approach to the various changes made during the course of its early life.

But most importantly, without the unconditional support of my wife Lorraine and her capacity to transcribe many of the tapes and to stay at home each night while I worked on the manuscript instead of doing other more important social things, there would be no book. She deserves my deepest thanks.

INTRODUCTION

Writing this book and talking with these widows has altered inexorably my perception of life, death and marriage.

The idea for the book took shape in my mind after two men died within a few months of each other. I had known them all my life and their widows made distinctly clear but very different observations about how they would spend the remainder of their lives. I began to examine the notion of singleness: how people deal with all the aspects of the death of a partner—male and female—and how their lives evolve after a short period and then, for those who choose not to take another partner, for a longer period, possibly the remainder of their own lives.

Widows, rather than a combination of widowers and widows, or simply widowers, are the subjects of the book for a number of reasons. Firstly, widowers—particularly younger men—tend to remarry fairly soon after the death of their partners. More often than not, they are also in a better financial position than widows, purely because the vast majority are in full-time employment. Older men, those already retired from permanent full-time employment, constitute the only group within the male population who tend to continue their lives either in the family home alone, or sell and move to a smaller apartment prior to moving into a retirement home.

Talking with the ten women who appear in this book, I have been moved by the strength they have shown, individually, in the face of utmost despair. Whether confronted by the spectre of three or four years of a partner's failing health, or whether their husband has died suddenly, they have had the capacity to draw from some unknown depth within themselves the ingredients to take control of their lives and the lives of their families and to embrace the future while holding on to a direct link to the past. This strength is not restricted to the ten women profiled here. It appears to be universal.

The women in this book range in age from 33 to 82. There was no attempt to make selections based on age, nor did I attempt to select women on the basis of circumstances. They were chosen because they were willing to tell their stories, willing to provide information—rather than advice—by way of anecdote, which they believe might be of assistance to other women in a similar situation.

There appears to be limited published information available and, as one younger woman remarked, the widows' societies and other organisations set up to help are pitched at the elderly. There is no support network for younger women other than family and friends.

The night before the final manuscript was due at the publishers, I watched television. A movie called *My Life* was on. It was about a bloke named Bob Jones who, unfortunately, was cast as a public relations practitioner. Bob Jones had a pregnant wife and he had been diagnosed with cancer. Early in the movie he discovered he had few friends. His wife suggested he see a Chinese medical practitioner. He bought a video camera and visited childhood haunts. Bob's video included a segment to his yet-to-be-born child about the possibility of his wife remarrying. It was the closest to reality that the movie came. Bob was quite unlike the picture of the husbands of the ten women who appear in these pages. Bob revisits his hometown and from there attempts to come to terms with his disease. In reality, most husbands are too busy putting in place those financial and physical structures which will provide their families with some assistance when they are no longer around.

While I found the inner strength of these ten women remarkable, it was their willingness to speak about their personal situations—their grief and how they dealt with a huge variety of issues—which has left an indelible print on my mind. Their collective self-effacement when confronted with the spectre of interview—of displaying publicly their innermost feelings on such a profoundly heart-wrenching subject—was also something I found extremely moving. All of them suggested their lives and their situations would be of little interest. Every one of them suggested I should go and find widows who had lived high-profile public lives. But these are not the people we relate to, other than in a fictional context. The ten women in this book, along with countless others in similar situations, are precisely those from whom we can gain most benefit by relating directly to their extreme circumstances. Very few of us benefit tangibly from watching Bob Jones running around with a video camera leaving shaving demonstrations for his unborn child, or seeing visions when attended by a Chinese medical practitioner. Where we do benefit is from the knowledge that there are other people in similar circumstances to our own who are confronting what appears to be insurmountable problems and pushing through. Jenny, with her three young children, knows she has the unconditional support of her family but she also knows she has to get on with her life. Her inner strength is profound. So is that of Helen who, even in old age, says she will just have to get on, despite losing her partner of almost 55 years. But get on with what? What is it that gives the appearance of forcing us to go on in the face of almost complete adversity? Reading these ten profiles of women faced with the reality which we all hope we will avoid, no matter what our age, financial circumstances or family, will, I trust, assist others in coming to terms with their own grief or at least provide a background which acknowledges that, no matter how difficult their personal circumstances, they are not alone.

ANNABELLE

Annabelle's story is one which examines the financial and social implications of the horror of sudden death. Annabelle puts on a brave face to the world, having lost her husband to a heart attack at 40. In the ten years since his death, she has attempted to maintain the lifestyle he gave her and their children. After years of being out of the workforce, she took any job she could get, travelled hours each day to work and made sure she was at home each evening to prepare meals for her children, to be there when they needed her. She now says life is pretty miserable without a partner but she has to keep doing what she is doing for the sake of the children. I was introduced to Annabelle through a mutual friend. She had been widowed for seven years and was still living in the home she and her husband had renovated, raising her two teenage children. Here she talks for the first time about her shocking discovery that her husband Alex had collapsed and died three doors from home one Sunday evening, while taking the dog for a walk. Annabelle said it took two years to recover from the shock of her widowhood at the age of 36. The strength she has found to continue to educate and nurture her two children is something she did not think she was capable of.

When I discovered Alex was dead all I could think of were very selfish things such as what's going to happen to me and who's going to look after the children? I had a lot of anger. I thought, how could he do this? I know this must sound awful, but I kept thinking, while I was at the hospital, who am I going to have sex with?

The night he died—it was the beginning of the Gulf War because he watched the news—he had been cooking dinner. He said he had indigestion and he was going to take the dog for a quick walk. We had just got this new dog. I mumbled something as he went out the door. Every Sunday since we had been married he would cook dinner for us. He went out and he was late back and I thought, where is he, why is he doing this? I thought I was going to have to finish the dinner. I was doing the ironing at the time and getting the kids ready for bed. The doorbell rang and when I answered it I saw the dog sitting there. It was the first thing I saw. Neighbours from down the road had hold of him. They told me straight away that Alex had collapsed. They suggested I leave the children next door. It was very confusing. I thought well, he had been working too hard—he was a broker and under a lot of stress but that was what he loved, he always said the stress was the best part of the job. Anyway, I took the children and left them next door. All the way to hospital—the neighbour who had brought the dog back drove me there—I thought oh, he's just been working too hard, that's all. I got to the hospital and they simply said, 'We're sorry, your husband has died.'

I couldn't even cry. I couldn't believe it. I was saying, 'But that can't be right. We were playing tennis earlier today. He's supposed to be at home cooking dinner.'

He had collapsed literally three doors from home. I just couldn't believe it. He was the only person I really knew. At the hospital they asked if there was someone I could call who would come and help me. I had no relatives here, so I called my closest girlfriend. She came straight away. My parents lived in Switzerland and Alex's lived in England so my girlfriend took me home. She collected the children and now I think about it she must have done everything there was to do. I can't remember much after I got home. All night I just stayed awake. I couldn't believe it.

I had to tell the children, which was the hardest thing in the world. They didn't appear to understand or believe what I was saying. But I just told them, look something awful has happened. I was 36 at the time, Alex was 40, Nicola was 10 and Ian was 7. That night, when I got home from the hospital, I just got into my bed and I took the children in with me.

When I went to the hospital, they told me I had to see him but I didn't want to. The nurse made me. She said I would regret it if I didn't. I just couldn't believe it. I suppose I was very selfish at the time—I thought, why is he doing this to me? I was so shocked. It seemed somehow very easy to tell the children. It was just a matter of saying that daddy had died, but I couldn't cry. I was with my neighbour in the waiting room when the doctor told me. I looked at the doctor but I was somewhere else; I was just thinking how could Alex do this to me? What about me? What's going to happen to me? I had too much pride to cry and I don't think I cried at all that night. Not even later, when the children were asleep. I just lay there hoping morning would never come.

I was in a complete daze for at least the first seven weeks. I thought he was coming back because he travelled a lot. For seven weeks I thought he was away and he was coming back. I had to go to the bank and do other normal things and my girlfriend, who was devoting all her time and attention to me and the children, said do this or do that. Her husband was also a great help. Two weeks after Alex died, they both came around and advised me on all sorts of financial things that I really hadn't thought about and had no intention of thinking about. I put a lot of trust in them, which was important because in the first two weeks after Alex died I had a lot of approaches from men coming around saying they could invest my money for me. I was very wary. They were men whom Alex had never trusted. He was a Scot and very careful; he was really a very distrusting man. He was very fond of a lot of people, but he knew some of them were up to no good. I remember him saying that if anything happened to him I should never trust so and so. Funnily enough, everything he said turned out to be right.

As time went on, it appeared his company had been in a bit of strife before he died. One day there was a knock on the door and I opened it to find a debt collector. I said, 'I don't know why you're here, my husband died seven weeks ago.' That was when it hit me. That was it. My attitude had always been well, we have to go on, but from that moment I rarely left the house for the next two years. I thought it was where I belonged and it was very hard to face anyone. I was even frightened to go to the shopping centre.

A lot of Alex's business friends ignored me and I was very hurt by that. He had a very small circle of friends and he had kept them for a long time. I think they ignored me because they didn't know what to say. I suppose that was fair enough. It was like having my right leg and my right hand cut off.

When I did find the nerve to go to the shopping centre, I experienced the same feeling I had had when my daughter was born. She was born in Japan and when I took her to the shopping centre I thought everyone was staring at me. It was the same thing all over again. So most of the time I couldn't bear going out because I thought everyone was going to stare. They weren't actually doing it but that's what I thought.

In the beginning it was very hard because I just didn't know what to do. I suppose I never thought it would happen to me, never. Alex had been a fit man. He was more health conscious than me even though he smoked. His father had had three heart attacks and he's still alive. That's why, at first, I couldn't believe it. Some time later I asked our family doctor if it was possible that I had contributed to his death. I felt guilty that maybe it was the food I had cooked all those years, but apparently not. You either have a blocked artery or you don't and it just happened. But it was such a shock. I still keep asking, no one in particular, why me? Why was it happening to me? Today, seven years later, I am actually much more aware of everything. I didn't realise there were so many nasty people around. I had been very, very protected in my home base. And I was very young. We were married when I was 21. I would have been married for 22 years if he had still been alive today.

We met at work. We were married and we did all our travelling together. We had no family around us but it didn't matter because we had each other. We did everything together. When the children were born we went to everything together; if we took our son to soccer, we went together. Now Alex is not here I wish I was geographically closer to my parents; it would be wonderful to ask my mum or dad to look after the children for a while. Everything we chose for the house, Alex and I chose together, but otherwise he mainly made the decisions. It was difficult to adjust to making decisions for myself and my children when all our married life Alex had made the important decisions for us. We lived in Japan for eight years before we moved here. Every decision was made by him when we returned. He bought the house knowing it was a good one. He always had a very good eye and he had very good taste; very good foresight; so I suppose I was happy with his decisions. This house is a typical example. After we lived in Japan I was very anti this place and I would argue against living here. It was a dump. But he knew it was the worst house in a good street. I couldn't see it. I wanted to move straight into something really nice. I've lived here for twelve years now.

Alex was right. I now have a strong asset. It's a lovely home. He had a very strong influence on our lives.

I think of him every day of my life. I dream of him a lot. Less and less, but the dreams are now becoming very strange. Because I have established my character, I don't want somebody to tell me what to buy any more. I want to buy what I want, which might not necessarily be as nice as he would have chosen, but it has been a way of establishing my own identity. This is what I want to do. During the past seven years there has really only been one thing that has been of the highest importance and that is protecting my children and being able to continue to look after them. I am investing a lot of time in their schooling because that is what Alex wanted. When I make a decision I still think gee, I wonder what Alex would have thought. A typical example was when I went to a trade fair and bought a cupboard. Alex would have bought a pair. That was how he operated. But I bought one and I could hear him behind me saying you've got to buy two but I was thinking no, I want one and this is it. It has been very hard to get used to making any sort of decision on my own but I think after seven years I am getting better at it.

Funnily enough, it was almost as if Alex knew something was going to happen because he kept saying he was not going to live past 40. He went to India when he was 20 and some Indian followed him down the street one day and told him strange things. He often told me he wasn't worried about anything because he was not going to be here after 40. And he wasn't. He never told me what the Indian said to him but I understand they believe that if you think you are going to die, you will. I don't think that is going to happen to me because I've got to look after the children. But he must have known something.

At the time of his death I wasn't working and I hadn't needed to work, other than at home, for thirteen years. So I had to go and get a job. I sat around the table, not many months after, with some friends and one of them said I should look for a job. I panicked. I had no confidence and I had no idea where to start. Who would want to employ me when, really, my secretarial and interpreting skills were not as good as they should have been? I decided the best place to start was voluntary work. I wasn't earning any money but it was an excuse to get out. I then got paid work which I had for four years.

Everything seemed to fall into place for a while. I don't know if it was because I was a woman. I think people were over-eager to help. Luckily no one took advantage of me except one man whom I now loathe. At the time I didn't know what I was doing. At one stage, two weeks after my husband died, I was prepared to give everything I owned to charity and to the Heart Foundation so I could find out what happened. A good friend advised me against that and I didn't do it, but at the time I didn't really care. I just didn't care about anything except the children. The worst instance of people wanting to help was when this man came and wanted to invest my money. He called himself an entrepreneur and I have since discovered he lost a lot of money over a few deals. My close friends knew about him and they were quite horrified. Even before the funeral he had come to see me, two or three days after Alex died. He came to the door and said I should trust him and that he would double my income. Just like that. I'd never heard of second mortgages. Alex looked after all our finances. But he had warned me about people like this and when I told certain people at the funeral they approached him and told him in no uncertain terms I was not interested.

I believe a lot of women who are widowed don't have friends they can turn to for financial or other advice. I have been very lucky. The two friends I trust with my finances knew Alex and how conservative he was and to me that has been an extremely big help. As time goes on I think I was very, very naive. When all this happened—this is how naive I was—I thought everyone had a home and everyone had money and savings. I got married very young to a man who was probably far more worldly wise than I was, so I thought everyone had children going to good schools. That's how naive I was. I also thought everyone had close friends who had homes and were renovating just like us. I thought that was all I needed.

I was never a religious person, not even when I was young, but I am totally against it now. If anyone asked me why, I would have to say that God has let me down. Why did he have to take Alex when he had two children to bring up? On the other hand, I think maybe it was for me. Maybe it was fate. Maybe God was telling me, come on, you can do it on your own. Some people have even said if this happened to them they would have their faith. I've got faith in myself. I think I can do just as good a job. I've got very good morals and principles. Going to church is not going to bring him back.

I was really angry with him for leaving me and for leaving the children. Totally angry. I found it very difficult to deal with it. I had counselling twice because my daughter and I were not getting on and I didn't want her to suffer. Both children hold a lot in but she just didn't talk much about it. We went to counselling but I didn't like the counsellor at all. I kept thinking that it was my responsibility, they were my children so it was up to me to make things better. If things went wrong at school I thought it was my fault. I know I shouldn't think like that but I couldn't help it. I've always felt like that. Probably because we've always lived away from my parents. I had the children and Alex had his job. My mother-in-law wouldn't come to the funeral because she couldn't face the fact that he had died before she had. She couldn't do it and I couldn't understand that. He wasn't one of my children but he was my husband and I couldn't understand her not coming.

My father came over from Switzerland and he was wonderful. We had seen him and my mother regularly over the years before Alex died. Today I wish I was living closer to them. I am only staying here basically because of the children and because I have a handful of friends. Acquaintances, I feel, have frittered away a bit because of my circumstances. Because I'm not married I'm seen as a threat to a lot of women. It gets a bit awkward. I get on extremely well with men because I like men. I don't have any bitterness towards men at all. There is a real difference, though, between friends and acquaintances. They're not all the same. I think without my two friends who I mentioned earlier, whom I trust, I would feel very vulnerable—towards men particularly. I am very happy to be in my home rather than being 'out there'.

Even though I'm now widowed I still think of myself as being married, especially when I go out. I certainly behave like a married woman, which certainly puts a few people off. They don't know how to handle that. I took my wedding ring off straight after the funeral. A lot of women thought that was awful but I don't know, I just had to. I wear it around my neck on a chain all the time. My first outing was after two years. When I finally left the house I was terrified. I was always hoping it was going to rain. I had not been out by myself without my husband for fifteen years. I didn't know how I could turn up anywhere. So my first outing was to a tennis match I had read about in the newspaper. My father told me to go. He said I couldn't stay in my kitchen for the rest of my life. I was hiding from everything. I thought, who wants to play tennis with me anyway? No one wants to know about a widow. I imagined everyone in the world had someone except me. Everybody had a husband or a boyfriend or partner and I didn't. So I went, but I discovered I was quite proud telling everyone I was a widow rather than divorced or single. It didn't matter to them at all. They couldn't see any difference between me and the other women. This sounds awfully vain but men would make advances, which really shocked me. The advances being made were quite shocking. A particular man put his tennis racquet between my legs. I said, 'Don't you ever, ever do that again to me.' They were all single and they were all out to find someone, whether it was for the night or what I didn't know. I was terribly naive and I still am, I think. Some single women would love that sort of attention. To them it may be a real turn on. From then on, the men didn't quite know how to handle me. I went to the club to play tennis, simply to get out of the house. I eventually met someone there whom I was very fond of. However, the whole time I went out with him I imagined him to be Alex. It was very difficult. I couldn't help but make comparisons with everything he did. At the beginning of that relationship I didn't really care because I thought, gosh, the first time I go out I meet someone, this is unbelievable. He was very different to Alex, though. He was very encouraging. He said I could do anything, whereas Alex would have said he was going to make the decision for us. In the relationship I had with him, for three and a half years, I thought he would take my son to the football, take us on picnics, that we would do everything together. That was my downfall, because we didn't. I kept thinking he was like Alex. But he was divorced and I now understand he was being very normal for a divorcee. He was totally independent whereas I was a total dependent. But it was someone. It was having someone around for a while. That was what was important. Acquaintances then started asking me around for dinner because there was someone in my life. We were a couple so it was not so embarrassing. It seemed that it was very hard to ask a single woman to dinner when there were only couples going to be there.

But that relationship stopped a few years ago. There hasn't been anyone since and it's been terrible because, when we finished, he—unbeknown to me at the time—married some-one else six weeks later and I couldn't believe he could do that. I suppose he must have been going out with her at the same time. I was shocked that a man could treat any woman like that because I don't think that way. Anyway, that broke up too, so she is also his ex-wife. I had only had one man in my life whom I had trusted 150 per cent and I really believed that every man was to be trusted, but obviously they are not. My single friends at that same tennis group had said, 'Oh Annabelle, you just don't realise.' And I hadn't. That's when they felt a lot of compassion towards me and I got a lot of support—from all of them. I eventually left that group because I couldn't cope with seeing him there all the time. And I couldn't cope with all the gossip. I don't like gossip.

In the end, though, I suppose he was a bit of a help. He was a very positive man. He told me, a lot of the times when I didn't get on with the children, how to deal with that. There has not been a weekend in seven years that I have not been without the children. I have them all the time and I can't understand someone who is divorced who complains because she doesn't have them all the time. When a divorced woman complains that she has her children every second weekend, that annoys me. He was very positive even though he didn't relate well to my children. He would say, 'Have you ever told your children that they are wonderful? Have you ever held them?'

I didn't get on well with my daughter, even from when she was a small baby. When Alex was around he would say it was my fault, that I was shouting at her, and he would say she would shout at me one day. And she does, but I think it is because we are very alike. Another friend said I should congratulate her for the good things she did rather than simply picking on her for the bad things, which I suppose we do as parents. I started doing that and I think it has made a big difference to our relationship. I don't know how I would have coped otherwise. As three people, I think we get on very well now, though it has been hugely difficult along the way. I am determined to keep that stability in the family. It is very high on my list. I treat them very much as adults. I don't ever leave them, whereas the divorcee would say 'get a life'.

Throughout the past seven years, I have been able to tell very clearly who my friends are. They are the friends I had when we were married. They are as solid as bricks. In the single world, it is so different because they are all fighting for their own space and their own relationships. There is a lot of competition. A lot of acquaintances who now ask me for dinner think I'm interested in their husbands, but I'm not. I'm more interested in the women as friends. It doesn't work that way, but I can't tell them what my thinking is. The single world is very different to married life. I realise now how stable and normal I was during my married life, but I don't think that is a good thing now: I was far too protected. I'm quite horrified how people behave. In the single world it seems to be that everybody keeps their options open, whereas in a sensible, stable relationship you can build a life with someone. When I was single I very much wanted to get married and to have children.

If I was to describe myself, I think I would say I am more of a communicator than a leader. I think I would probably go along with things. I like having someone to share things with. That's what I miss. My children have been a godsend because they keep me going. I went to a widows' association in the beginning and I found it so depressing. It was all older women who couldn't see any future. They were all in their fifties and sixties. Their view on life was awful. One woman had taped her bedroom shut, never to be opened again, and her husband had died five years before. The objective of the association was to get together to share experiences, but I realised the reason why they were so depressed was that their children had grown up and they only had four walls to look at. All the plans they made fell apart because suddenly they were unemployable, they had no one and there appeared to be no point in going on. They didn't know what to do on their own, whereas at least I had the advantage of being young enough to go and get another life. I know now more or less where I want to go. To do something if I want to. My purpose in life at the moment, however, is to be here for my children. Some people have mentioned that I should get a foster father for Ian but I've said no, I can cope. I can take him to the football and do things with him. Probably the most difficult thing in a relationship with two children is that you have to consider them all the time, especially a young boy. He doesn't like it if I go out for dinner or anything. He is very much at home here and I encourage that. I say you are the man here and I want you to fix this or that. He is 14, whereas my daughter, at 17, is much more competitive with me. She's got me to fight with, which is a good outlet for her.

I have now progressed through the workforce, very slowly, from voluntary to part-time to full-time, but five years ago things were much easier. I don't know if it's because I was new on the scene. Now I have to fight for a lot more. I can cope financially, but my biggest dread is that I will spend my money on something stupid and that I will have to keep working, or lose my home, or not be able to afford to send the children to school. That is the biggest dread in my life because whenever things went wrong I used to look at Alex and think everything would be all right. I had him around and he would just work harder to make more money, or whatever. It is a real worry, although I'm very, very careful with money, especially with what I spend on the children, very frugal. My daughter will probably want a car one day, so I have to think about trying to save for that now. On the other hand, because I am a little bit careful, I can imagine I am going to be too careful and I am going to die and not spend anything. But that's fine because the children will get it. What was left to us was security because I had the house. I don't wander around thinking I won't be working at some stage in the future. I thoroughly enjoy it. Because I felt so useless for the first two years, I now have a purpose and work is part of it.

Never needing to consider remarrying is one of the hardest things to explain. It is really difficult to explain to someone who is divorced and bitter about men that you've had a good marriage for fifteen years and if you never marry again it doesn't matter. No one can live up to Alex. No one could be as well mannered and no one could be as caring for us. It's because he was the father of my children. Five years ago I was looking for a replacement father for them, which was wrong. At 17 and 14 I think they are too old to accept someone as a new father. I'm more interested in simply having company, for them and me. If it were to happen, I would not be averse to having a long-term relationship, but I am not interested in one-night stands. You look more along the lines of company, if you look. I think the children, particularly, are probably happy the way things are. I'm probably the one who gets a bit down because I am with them all the time and I can't seem to always be splitting myself into being two people for them. Most of the time I can cope, but there are times when it is depressing.

I think, in the beginning, when I first started going out, I put too much emphasis on how the children would feel about who I was going out with. Would they approve? Everybody who came into my life was compared to Alex—as a father and as a husband. It was very difficult. Three of my girlfriends also did that, made comparisons. They were very open in saying they didn't like who I was going out with. When they did that it also touched me. Now seven years later I think, well, am I trying to please my children and my friends or am I trying to please myself? I suppose the difficulty is trying to strike a balance—a balance for them and for me.

It's becoming a lot easier to talk about the whole thing, but I still think about Alex every single day of my life and I think it's partly because I still live here, in the home we made together. He will always be with us. He was a very, very good person. The single men I meet leave their options open. I keep thinking there has got to be at least one stable man like him. If someone were to say to me OK, you've had seven years of single life, what would you prefer, I would go back to what I had, but that's me. A lot of the time I wish things were just as they were but I know they never will be. It's a very different type of grieving when you know someone has gone, completely gone, than when you have finished a relationship and you know that person is still around, still in existence. That's worse. You feel like really telling them off because of how awful they've been. I think that's one of the reasons I want to stay in this house because it holds me to Alex. It's very hard to describe how one should deal with grief. I suppose you just go on. Having children makes you go on.

Alex was cremated. It was extraordinary because three weeks before he died I told him about a girlfriend whose husband had died in an accident on the highway and he asked what the funeral arrangements were. I said she hadn't wanted a big funeral and Alex said he thought that was a bit mean. Then he said something unusual. He said I shouldn't worry: if I wanted to have a big funeral when he died, I should go ahead and do it. This may sound awful, but at the funeral I had so much attention. I couldn't believe the amount of attention I had. I didn't know what was happening. My father organised everything. I actually thought at the funeral that Alex was there and that he was waiting for me outside. The children went to the funeral and my father thought it was the wrong thing to do. Ian didn't cope with it very well. He was very quiet. He has oodles of common sense. When he does something he always says his dad showed him how. He was only seven and he now knows how to fix things. I have a lot of self-discipline and I now want a good time, but I think I hold back. To a lot of single women today that is crazy. They say no, you've got to go out and get a life. My daughter tells me to get a life but I don't want to. I think she'd like to be in charge.

I remember thinking, when we were first married, when I walked into my living room, that if only I were on my own here all this would be mine. When it happens though, you find you are very lonely. I have changed the furniture around since Alex died. With my friends. They helped. I changed it around because I wanted my colours in here, just for me, but it still doesn't change the house. Anything that was specifically Alex's I have left.

Even if I never marry again it doesn't matter, because we had fifteen years where some people only have two, or even one. Although I hope I don't spend the rest of my life alone. If my children or my friends didn't like someone, that would put me off. I'm very fussy. I would like to meet someone in their mid-forties or fifties and they're pretty rare. Someone said I would have to look at an older age. Younger men do play a lot of games trying to make you jealous and I can't be bothered with that. I have met a few widowers, which is interesting. One I quite liked. He was a very nice man and someone prompted me, urged me, to call him. I could never call a man, not my generation and they said if I didn't someone else would get him. He was 50 and someone else has got him now, but that's fine. He found someone else within eight or nine months of his wife dying. That is probably the difference between a man and a woman. A woman is very much more conscious of what her friends are going to think if she gets a man within six months, whereas a man doesn't care. He will get a woman and no one is going to say anything about him. It's a bit like the idea that a man can have a lot of women and be told he's cool, whereas a woman can have a lot of men and she'll be told she's a tart.

I often thought if I had been the one who died, how would my husband have coped with lunchboxes? Children? What do you wear to school? In my children's eyes, things changed very little. I was still here to do all that and I still do it, whereas a man is very much focused on his job. If a man is left with two or three children what is he going to do? He only knows his job and he wants the company of a woman. A man can't seem to be without a woman for very long. Not only to have around to wash up the dishes and do the ironing for him, but for company, whereas I think a woman is much stronger.

I never thought I would have the strength I have at the moment. You get lonely but you feel strong because you have to be. Strong mentally. I have to be strong in front of the children. I very rarely let myself down because if I show weakness they don't see me in the right light. If I said I was lonely and I hated being on my own, they might think it was their fault, whereas it has had nothing to do with them. I've built a bit of a wall around me. I want a man who has manners, just like Alex. I compare a lot to him, although I have moved away from that in the past couple of years. The difference between me and my married friends is that they go out, and I go out, but then they go home and close their bedroom door and they are together. I go home and I am on my own and I think gee, that was great going out but what now? My single friends who are divorced or separated understand what it is all about. In all fairness to my friends, I would have been exactly the same. I would have had Alex to go home with and I would have said, oh poor girl, oh well, and we would have gone home and we would have talked about the party and would have planned what we were going to do tomorrow. The point is, we would have been doing it together.

The two-year point after Alex's death was an important milestone. For about two years it didn't bother me that I had no one in my bed. One of the things that went through my mind in the hospital was the question of who I would have sex with. Isn't that terrible? I thought about the kids and everything else but I also questioned who would want me. I was quite horrified at my own thoughts. Alex and I didn't have a very physical relationship, but it didn't matter. It was a marriage. He was an excellent provider. He was trustworthy. I don't think he ever had anyone else and I know I certainly didn't but it didn't matter and for two years I wasn't looking for sex at all. If I was going to have that, it was going to be with someone I really wanted to be with, who wanted to be with me.

When I met the man I mentioned earlier, it was very different. I actually didn't know how to cope with it. Later on, he said I talked about Alex a lot but he was very understanding. He had never been out with a widow before. The physical aspect with him was very different to when I was married and I think if I meet a man today, or if I have a date, I have a terrible feeling that that's what he wants and that's all. I think sex is very important for a lot of men my age and I think that's very sad. With the man I mentioned, I went out with him for three months before anything happened and I think he was quite shocked. It was a bit of a challenge for him, I guess. I am no different today. When I meet a man of my age, or in his fifties, he's a little bit bitter towards women. And I think that's all they want and I'm very disappointed. I can go out with a man two, three or four times and after the fourth time they get quite nasty.

Recently I had a bad experience where a man spent quite a bit of money on food when we went out. But it just wasn't working out and he shouted at me and said I was negative but that was because I didn't fancy him at all. There was no chemistry, but I did like the man. I thought he was interesting. However, he wanted more. It's very sad. I was actually quite terrified because I thought he was going to hit me. He had spent the whole night looking at some other woman.

He was 50 and he had never married. He told me during the evening he was having psychological help because he could never hold a relationship and I listened, but there was no chemistry. I suppose I shouldn't have gone, but I had nothing else to do that evening. I really love adult company but I realised then that the poor man was not getting what he wanted out of it so he turned nasty. He shouted at me in the car and said nothing could please me. I said he had it all wrong but I couldn't wait to get out of the car and I burst into tears because I'd never met men like this before.

I met Alex when I was 19, married him at 21 and we had children when I was 26. My whole life was with him and he had never treated me like that. I must have come from a very protected little world. On this basis I think my female friends have been a lot more precious to me than my male friends. To me, sex is very precious. Even though it was not a big thing in my marriage I suddenly realised if you have a good marriage, that there is so much more. Alex was an excellent husband and a good provider and he loved his children and he cared for me and looked after us even when he died. This is the depth of a marriage. The first relationship I had after it seemed to be all physical. When I broke up with that man I went out on a few dates and I realised it didn't matter what profession they were in, that was all they wanted.

The men I get on with best are happily married—I think because I was there myself and when they talk about their wives I know what they are talking about because I was like that. I think they are comfortable in their relationships so they are comfortable with me. They are no threat and I am no threat. Once when I went out, a man asked if he could buy me a drink and I said I was a lot more interested when he had his wedding ring on. He had taken it off when he had earlier left the table. He would have been far more interesting to talk to if he had been married.

A widow could never trust anyone in her life and have a really boring time. I knew one widow who died when she was 55 and she had never trusted a man. She told me not to when I was first widowed and in a way she was right, but she never had any fun because she was constantly protecting what she had and she became paranoid. If I was 70 I think I'd just go for it. I became very distrustful after that first relationship and I am still wary, but I do trust men a lot. But if I don't trust a man, I don't think I'll never go out again or that I'll never have any fun. And I don't want to do that. Life is a gamble now.

A lot of the time when I make decisions, I wonder what Alex would think of them. That's a very sobering thought. It occurs to me when I'm being foolish or I'm angry with the children—my daughter's very like him, she answers me back and I think gosh, you're just like your father. I have his pictures all over the family room and I think it's probably difficult for a man to come into my life when Alex is everywhere. I have to think of me now, rather than what the children think, even though I still have to consider them. If they were not happy, a relationship for me would never work.

Being a widow hasn't stopped me taking the children to see my parents in Switzerland and Alex's parents in England. We went to Bangkok too, although I still miss Alex to travel with. It's not something I can do easily. I don't think having money makes any difference if there is no one to share it with. I would rather have Alex.

If one day I wake up and I don't know where the next meal is coming from, it will be my fault for not managing my money very well or for frittering it away. I get sick of people saying I am lucky because I have a house. What do they mean by lucky? I'm not lucky. Money cannot buy you what you want and you learn that the hard way. The thing I like about myself now is that when I meet a man I don't cling on. I actually don't need them. I might want them but I don't need them for stability and I don't need them for money because I am totally independent. When it comes to my kids' schooling, I am not looking for a man to pay for it. That is entirely my responsibility and I think me being the type of woman I am, I am going to feed them and house them, and that is my whole responsibility.

It's only now after seven years I feel the loneliness creeping in more. Although I can talk to the children, they are still children and I think, I have worked all day, I come home and get dinner and cope with their problems and their ups and downs and then I go to bed because I am so tired. I don't care what I do. It doesn't matter about me as long as they are happy. As a woman, as I get older, I think if I go on leaving it am I never going to meet anyone again, but the best thing to do is not to concentrate too much on it. It would be nice but it's not a big deal.

I am so glad I am in the workforce. I would encourage a lot of women who are married to get back into the workforce at least by the time they are 40 because if some disaster happens to them at least they are more able to cope with it. It is so hard to get back in, but it gives you confidence. On this basis I don't like weekends very much because they are concentrated so much on the children. I have a social tennis group on Saturday afternoon, but that's all. Saturday night I am usually here with my son and Sunday is taken up with washing the car and other domestic chores. I don't like Sundays very much because I am usually by myself. A lot of my married friends are with their families and they are probably the people I want to see most, but I feel obliged to be at home with the children. I might take the kids to the beach and we will have an early dinner but it is basically all children because I feel I should be with them. During the week I get up at 6 o'clock and start getting them ready for school. Then I go to work till 5 o'clock. I'm home at 5.30. Monday night is food shopping; Tuesday night is cleaning; Wednesday night is with the children; Thursday night I might go out for dinner. Flexible shopping hours are wonderful for me, although funnily enough now I am far more organised than when I had so much time to do everything. I had all day to shop then and I would think, what have I done all day? Whereas now it is like clockwork. I can zip around the supermarket in half an hour. I suppose in that regard it is a lot easier for me than for a married woman because I only have my children to contend with. I don't have the pressure of a woman who works full-time plus has a husband and children. She has a lot more to do than I do. I come home and it doesn't matter what we have for dinner. It might be bacon and eggs, whereas a man would question having his traditional breakfast at dinner time. I don't have that stress. I may not even eat some nights. I play tennis some Thursday nights and again in competition on Friday nights but I feel a bit guilty when I go out. But I love my tennis. It takes my mind off things.

Because I am on my own, I think I don't want to live to an old age. If I was still married or living with someone else, it probably wouldn't bother me. I used to think about it a lot and expect a lot just after Alex died, but now I take every day as it comes, although I do have ambitions now. I would love to have my own coffee shop. I really want a new car someday. I would like to see the children through their schooling without too much drama before I do that because they will take up a lot of time. I don't worry about the risk of going into business. It is the first time in my life I want to do something for me. I always did everything for Alex. Which was fine.

I wouldn't have been doing this or thinking about a business in the future if he was still around. He would have said I should examine the figures. I would have done what he wanted me to do. His business was very important and I always felt good helping him with it. I was always behind him, entertaining for him. Suddenly I have been given all this freedom but I don't really want it. I felt when I told the children that their father had died that very little changed in their lives because their lunch was made, they went to school and I wasn't working so I was always there for them. Once when my son and I were searching for something, we looked under his bed and I noticed in a book he had a photo of his father. Then I looked in one of his little chests and he came through the door and he was very upset. He said I should never look in there again. If I can keep my children stable and keep loving them, it is better for them, even if it's not good for me. I will be here always for them. I think it is less disturbing for them than having a father they see every two weeks, like they might if we were divorced. What I don't understand is that Alex was much healthier than me. He just knew he was going to die. It was extraordinary. When he was twenty the Indian man shouted at him and one of the things he said was that he knew Alex's girlfriend's name was Annabelle and it was true. I think he was haunted all his life by that.

The last night Alex and I were together was at a friend's place. He loved good clothes, good wine, good food, good crystal glasses and laying the table then sitting down to an elegant dinner. On our last night together we had dinner at a friend's place and it was just how he loved it. He was well dressed and he had made the soup and we had very beautiful wine. My girlfriend said later, it was amazing, that night was just how he loved to live. It was just unbelievable. That's how he set it up. That's how he loved to eat and live and we had a fabulous evening and the next day he was gone and that's something I will never, ever come to terms with.

GILLIAN

Gillian's story is one of anguish and heartbreak. It is the story of a woman who showed strength and courage when her husband, after almost twenty years of marriage, left her for a younger woman only to come home to die. It was just before Christmas. Gillian's husband Stephen was out to dinner with friends and associates from work. They were having dinner in a restaurant and after they had eaten, they got up to dance. Stephen was known to dance in a fairly energetic manner but on this occasion he dropped to the ground, dead. Gillian spoke to me frankly about the process of grieving and about the stress of living with a partner who had been diagnosed with heart problems but was unable to confront them on a day-to-day basis.

The night Stephen died, I had taken our children to a show in town. The dinner he went to was impromptu—he and his work associates were celebrating a business contract they had won. My daughter was 16 at the time and my son was 14. I was 40. He had told me he was going to have a celebratory dinner with some people from work. He had asked me if I could go, but I had already arranged to take the children out.

When I got home at around 11 o'clock, the telephone rang and it was one of the people from work to say Stephen had had some sort of collapse. She said he was in hospital and that they would come and pick me up if I could get someone to stay in the house with the children. I managed to organise that and the friends from work arrived and drove me to the hospital. He was dead. They had not told me. They knew because he died as he fell on to the dance floor. The paramedics had pronounced him dead and taken him straight to hospital.

When I arrived at the hospital, a doctor came out and explained to me how Stephen had died. I said I would like to see him, but there had to be a post-mortem because the doctors at the hospital did not know his history. They could not sign a death certificate without a post-mortem. I had to have a policeman present when I saw him. I had to wait for half an hour or so for the police. They were very kind. Everyone was waiting. The chaplain waited with me. They were all devastated. It was like slow motion. There was no post-mortem in the end. It was 3 o'clock in the morning and I went into numbness. I didn't cry. I was just cold. I'm a practical person and I think that helped.

I remember thinking it was very important that I saw him then because I was never going to believe it. I knew it was difficult for everybody when I said I wanted to see him, but I just had to. When I touched him, he was already cold.

My friends then drove me home and I had another friend who was there and she stayed with me. My son wasn't home because I had arranged for him to stay with some other friends. My daughter was at home asleep and when she woke up in the morning, I told her. I didn't sleep that night. I didn't sleep properly for years. I can't remember how I told my daughter: her reaction was a bit like mine.

Looking back, I can't over-emphasise how shocked we were and what shock does to you. I look at the two years after he died and I think I was in shock the whole time. I can't remember much about that whole period and in a sense I don't have a clear picture of day-to-day life at all. It was like when you swim underwater and you make a lot of automatic movements with your arms and your legs but your hearing and your sight are blurred. You are unaware of your own weight. I know I kept going to work. Stephen died at the beginning of the school holidays—I worked as a school teacher—so I had to be patient, but I remember I just couldn't wait to get back to work. Then I just went through the motions. God knows what I was like to work with. Although I think I did an OK job, I was quite unconscious of what was happening to anyone else. I was just getting myself through each day. I thought I was doing fine but it must have been awful for everyone around me. I was oblivious to it all.

We had known since he was 36 that Stephen had a heart problem and it had been a huge shock then to find that out. He had always suffered from heartburn. He had a commercial pilot's licence but when he went to have his medical each year, no problems had shown up. He thought it was indigestion. Our family doctor said he should stop eating all fatty foods. Eventually it did get to the point where it was worrying him, so a friend who was also a general practitioner actually did some intensive tests. He then had more tests with little electrodes rushing around his body and they discovered that he actually had some blocked arteries. The conclusion was that he would probably do well to have a heart bypass, but they said he didn't need to do it immediately. They said the longer he waited the better the technology would be, so he continued doing what he had been doing, without the fatty foods.

At first, when he was told about the heart problems, he was shocked and he became very careful. We did the diet thing and the cholesterol thing and we did the exercise thing but it didn't last and I think he actually went into denial. He then went through a process of covering it up. He threw his drugs away because they made him feel sick. He said he wasn't going to take them because he had a highly paid executive job to do. When he died ten years later, and for the whole period of time since, my grieving has been affected by an extraordinary level of guilt. What has happened since was so directed by what happened before he died that it is very enmeshed.

I say he was in denial after he was diagnosed because he kept on finding extraordinary things to do. It was as if he had to find a final mountain to climb. First of all he decided he didn't want to be an engineer any more, he wanted to be a doctor. He had always wanted to be a doctor so he tried to get into medicine at university, but they could not admit him to the course unless he sat for the high school exam so he said he would and he went to technical college at night and he did it. This was the late 1970s. I went back to teaching permanently in 1979. The kids were little and my salary wasn't much, as I was teaching part-time. Well, he missed out on medicine by a few marks. He said, 'Bugger that, I'll do it again.' So he did it again and he still missed out by two marks and still they wouldn't let him in. In the meantime, of course, we had forfeited holidays because he needed the time to study. I think he was actually a little mad by then. In fact, thinking back, he was in quite a mad state because of the heart condition. I don't think there was any other reason.

We had been living in a rented house that was to be resumed for an expressway, so we thought we had better build a house. We financed a block of land with another block we owned. Stephen then designed and built the house—this was the next mountain to climb. It took two or three years because he subcontracted the building out. When it was finished, he had an affair with another woman and left home for two years. I moved into the house and he moved away. I think this was also part of the heart condition and partly a mid-life crisis, but he had all these reasons to have a crisis. The heart thing added to it, plus the fact that he failed to do his medicine. Mind you, in one way I was glad he hadn't got in because we would have been unable to live adequately. It was a dream. He met the other woman at work—'the secretary', really clichéd stuff, so you can imagine how absolutely furious I was—I was ready to kill at that stage but it was actually extraordinarily sad. It is a terribly debilitating thing when your partner walks off with someone else—just about every doubt you ever had about yourself seems to be confirmed; you are completely stripped of your confidence.

I was married very young and I think that had a lot to do with my loss of confidence. Stephen was very much the 'knight on white horse with shining armour and drawn sword'—that sort of admiration. We got married younger in those days but I was particularly young, which greatly worried my parents, but it was fine. I mean, it appeared to be fine for thirteen or fourteen years. In the end it was traumatic for me and eventually for Stephen. It was hard for Stephen's parents as they were very conservative and I think they lost a lot of respect for him when he left me for another woman. At that point he had a job change and moved interstate to be with his girlfriend. He thought it would be a clean start.

The saddest thing was the change in his relationship with his children. Our daughter was just starting high school and she was devastated when he finally decided to move out. After all the covering up for the children's sake, I finally lost my temper and made him go and tell them himself. I remember they were both desperately upset and my daughter just said, 'Nothing will ever be the same again.' He doted on her and he destroyed their relationship right there and then. My son was much better. He was devastated, but he was younger. He thought his father was a god and he somehow kept that faith. He cried and he cried but he didn't lose faith in his 'Dad'.

So Stephen went away and there was the usual strained relationship. He missed the children like mad. At one stage the children went to stay with him. They said they would stay with him but only if the girlfriend was not there, so it all became very difficult. That was a nightmare period in my life. Eventually it all came crashing down around his ears because his new young partner just couldn't understand him. He was a very complicated man. She couldn't put up with the sadness he felt about his children. She eventually got herself a new boyfriend and from then on his dependence on me was extraordinary because he would ring me up—quite suicidally—late at night, which was a terrible process. He was very hurt by it all. He had compromised his relationship with his parents. He had gone a long way to ruining his relationship with his daughter and he had completely shattered me. No wonder he was depressed.

He eventually came back, though. He suggested to me he wanted to start a company selling a product that he had discovered, basically spinning off some technology that he thought he could make some money out of. He thought the company he was working for was not selling it particularly well and he saw a niche in the market. He said he would come back and try to set it up and I thought this was the most positive he had been since the heart diagnosis. So he came back and he lived elsewhere and he started his company. He sold his car and started the company on $12 000. It was hard work and there was no money at first. He shared office space with a friend at minimal rates, used an old computer and got to work. Even though he wasn't with me, all the time he had been supporting the kids. At that stage I was head of the English department at my school and on as much money as I could earn. Both kids had ended up at private schools and we had a mortgage I couldn't cope with. He paid that and something towards the school fees. He also maintained my car, which was wonderful. He used to come around like a dog with his tail between his legs and say he would fix the car and I would say that maybe I would give him a cup of tea. It was a bit sad really, because I was cruel to him.

I don't think you ever get over the death of your husband. I think you just learn to live with it. I still get times when I get incredibly weepy about the whole thing. Even though I didn't shed tears the night he died, I did an awful lot of crying from there on. I did what I called carweeping. I did that for at least a year and then intermittently for another two or three years. It was part of changing roles between home and work. It took me about half an hour to get to work. I'd get in the car and I'd cry all the way. I'd get there, park the car and dry my eyes, then I'd get out and turn into an English teacher—head of the department. In the afternoon I'd get back in the car and I'd weep all the way home. Carweeping was probably the only opportunity I had to be unobserved by my children or work associates—when I was on my own, unidentified in the traffic.

When your husband dies, you can't do very much about the sexual side of the relationship except to miss it, unless you're going to hang around in singles bars. I don't think it becomes less important, but I think you make it become so because that's the way you have of dealing with it. Like the death of your partner—you don't get over it, you learn to live with it. I think the thing you miss more than the actual sex is the intimacy, the touching. You're starved in a tactile way. It's the intimacy of an everyday relationship that you miss. But you cope with it. It probably changes your personality, but it's hard to work out how. I can't judge myself.

He came back in 1985 and for about eighteen months of the two years he was back, before he died, we decided to try to pull the marriage back together and he came home. Reconstituting a marriage is not something you take on lightly and it was not a happy process. Even though he was starting his business—which was a hard struggle because nothing seemed to be happening—it was not very successful because he was still deeply depressed. We were essentially just living in the same house together. We had a very good physical relationship early on in our marriage, but this had been killed. It made it almost impossible and part of the problem was his constant desperate depression. Even though he had a new challenge and he rose to it, it only occupied his working days.

I believe now—and this is why I felt so guilty—that he was clinically depressed. I think he needed treatment. He couldn't sleep. He drank too much wine, although he was never drunk in the house. This is where it haunts me because I didn't seem to be able to do anything to make him feel better about anything. I think that the only joy he had was when he and our son went bike riding or to car races; they did things fathers and their boys do. Just before he died, a couple of big orders had come in and he realised the company would get going and then, suddenly, he died. Only a few months before, I had been encouraging him to go to his heart specialist and be reviewed because I noticed he couldn't walk up the back stairs without puffing and without pain. I know he couldn't go bike riding with our son without pain. Eventually he went to the doctor. He came home and said the doctor had wanted to wait a bit longer—it was all right. I now know he did not tell the heart specialist the truth. I couldn't have gone with him because our relationship was such that he wouldn't let me. He was in total denial.

I was never really a religious person. In fact, it was work that got me through the whole trauma. My daughter was going through a very religious phase at that stage which was very good in one way, because her church friends gathered around her and saw her through it. That was wonderful for her. On the other hand, because of their narrow view of things, she said, 'Daddy will go to hell', and I had to sit her down and say that if she believed in God, what sort of a God was he if he would do that? I had to have that talk with her a lot of times because she had suffered guilt as I had. All of a sudden he was dead and we both had so much unfinished business. It was just terrible. All I felt, and I still feel to some extent, was guilt.

I look back on that period before he died with great regret. I mentioned earlier about wanting to see Stephen when he died, but in subsequent days, before the funeral, I made sure that the children saw him as well. I asked them—I wanted them to see him, and I asked them if they'd like to and they said they wanted to. Both have commented since that they are glad they did. Particularly when my daughter went to the Middle East for the first time. One of the things she wrote back to me about—it was absolutely horrible—was that she thought she saw her father on the streets the whole time. Although he had no Middle Eastern ancestry, he had broken his nose playing football as a kid and it was a little bent and his features were slightly Jewish, with a moustache and dark hair. She just kept seeing him everywhere. So seeing him when he had died had been important.

I was christened Church of England. So was Stephen. My grandfather was a canon in the Church if England. We went to the local Presbyterian Church when the children were young and going to Sunday school, but the first sermon was all fire and brimstone and we were all heading for hell. At the end of the service we came out and Stephen said, 'I'm never going in there again.' We just couldn't make it real. It just didn't work for us. Yet Stephen had a Christian burial which was mainly due to my daughter and her connections with the church. There was a burial and a memorial service as stated in both Stephen's and my will. The reason we decided to be buried was simply that it seemed better to have a place which we could associate with the person, rather than a plaque on a wall and I must say I'm glad we did that. It's not an easy service to get through but it is probably useful from the grieving point of view because it is very final. A burial is so confronting. It's tangible. Much more so than a cremation. I visit the cemetery occasionally.

People used to ask me if I felt angry and I would say, 'No, definitely not.' I had got over my anger with him for the affair with the young woman. All I felt was this incredible sadness that he hadn't been happier. That he hadn't reconstituted much that meant anything to him in that last year or so. At the time of his affair, I had two children to look after so God knows how they would have felt if I'd had another relationship. They were already devastated. Anyway, I wasn't interested. Frankly I had had it with men at that stage and nothing was further from my mind. I was intent on looking after my children. I wasn't angry when Stephen died. I am sure at some level there is anger, but anger was simply not part of that period of my life. Sometimes Stephen would show anger or desperation due to what was happening to him, but mostly it was just overwhelming guilt that he had spoiled everything. He was more angry with himself.

Part of the reason I have never tried to run a relationship with anyone else in these past ten years is that he was a hard act to follow. He was not only tall, dark and handsome but incredibly intelligent, funny, witty and urbane. He could talk to anyone and was interested in everything. He did interesting things. He was an extraordinarily good companion. I don't think I'll meet his like again. So the sadness and the guilt are all to do with the fact that the last couple of years of his life he was just such a changed personality. He was dead before he fell, metaphorically.

I think there are only three kinds of men. The worthwhile ones are well and truly accounted for. The others who are nice are gay, and what you have left after that are creeps. There is a small group whose wives don't understand them. You can imagine how much patience I've got with them. I happen to believe their wives understand them very well, thank you very much. I'm just not interested in such relationships. It's highly unlikely I will establish another long-term relationship. There are not a lot of the right kind of men available. I think the reason I don't meet men who might be available is because I don't really try to. Perhaps I don't want to, or maybe I'm far too fearful. I'm amazed at the number of women who do, though. Some marry immediately afterwards, only to end up unhappy. I was very lucky that my husband's company went on to be quite successful with a friend who steered it through, before liquidation, to make some money. Not all of the money came to me, but a substantial amount did and that's invested. As far as I'm concerned it's the children's inheritance. That has made our lives much easier. I did not have to struggle with financial problems as many widows do.

I grew up in the country. Originally my father had a property in the far northwest where I grew up before coming to the city to attend boarding school. I was five years behind the rest of my family and grew up in quite a solitary way and I think that has had an effect on how I am now, in adult life. I think I was quite a solitary child. I come from a very practical family. It was made pretty clear to my sister and me, when we were little, that there wasn't enough money, and with brothers who needed the property, we were going to have to get ourselves a career, so we did. Which was a bit sad in a way and sexist. The sons would be on the land and the girls were going to have to get on with it.

It was through my sister, who is six years older than me, that I met my husband. Her boyfriend, whom she eventually married, and Stephen were very good friends. Her husband and Stephen went to school together and they used to fly together. We spent a lot of our time together until Stephen went off to live in Melbourne after university. When he came back we went out for about six months before we got married. He was 25 and I had my head completely turned.

He was the most positive and electric person. He had a glamorous job with an airline doing performance studies on jumbo jets. This also involved many overseas journeys. He changed to mining engineering after we married. He took a job with a major mining company out west and they provided us with a huge house. We'd never had a house. They paid our electricity and telephone bill and gave us wood for the winter and they paid him a good deal of money. For us it was amazing. It was fun out there, as that particular mine was the most advanced in the Southern Hemisphere at the time. It attracted many young professional people, so life was fast and full. He always had successful jobs so the early part of my marriage was good.

Friendship is an interesting topic. It's very muddy because we separated for some time so friends at that stage changed.

People who had originally been his friends didn't know what to do with their hands at that point. Some, certainly, were trying to be even-handed and that was complicated enough. When he came back he was so depressed and so difficult that we actually didn't see anyone. We didn't have anyone here. It was deadly. I had started another circle of friends, from work or associated with work, and they helped me through the separation, but they were not his friends. This network of friends was very important to me because I felt betrayed by other friends in some ways. People who were Stephen's friends just faded away at the time we were separated. If not then, they certainly faded when he died. A lot of people came to the funeral. I didn't see many of them afterwards—especially a lot of people who were supposed to be his friends. I thought even if they don't particularly like me, they might pay some attention to the children. Perhaps they were too uncertain to approach us. I used to go to dinner and the theatre with one group of friends, but I gave it up after a little while as they couldn't seem to allow me my independence. I was now a women on her own, through widowhood. Some well meaning but paternalistic man always wanted to pay for me which made me feel very uncomfortable. My mother died the same year as Stephen so it was a truly miserable year. She had Alzheimer's disease and she was getting worse leading up to Stephen's death, which was another thing to cope with. It made me very tired. They lived in the north-west so I'd drive up every third weekend or so to help my father.

The relationship I have with my children has always been close but I think it just got closer. They fought like brothers and sisters do when they were younger, but now they are quite good friends. My son lives in Hong Kong now and my daughter is based in Oxford at the moment. I've been to Hong Kong a couple of times to see my son and to England to see my daughter. She is an archaeologist so she is off on digs around the Middle East most of the time. When she lived here for twelve months last year with her boyfriend, we had a good relationship. We lived happily together. I don't know how I would have existed without the children. They kept me sane. They were the reason I stopped crying when I got out of the car in the afternoon. They have been an entirely positive influence and an endless source of interest and satisfaction.

I come from a family which tends to live a long time and I will probably keep working provided there is something interesting for me to do. I'm interested in developing consultancy work and if it is interesting and fun it's good to work. I don't have a relationship, but I really miss the idea of having one. What I want is a 'call-up lover' who will go travelling overseas with me and have the odd weekend away. When you don't have a companion who you can do things with, it is important to work as long as you can as it makes you feel as if you're doing something useful and that there is a reason to be alive.

Until I made a major investment decision and bought a block of land on which I built a holiday cottage, I had sort of limped along. That's the other thing you want a 'call-up lover' for, someone who would be waiting around to take the blame in case you make the wrong decision. The thing that is really irritating, for women who have had someone to talk things over with, is learning to make all the decisions on your own. That's the thing I find most difficult about living alone—like what to do about the car, deciding whether I should sell it when it wears out or even knowing if it is worn out or if I need a new one. Even if the advice is wrong, at least there is someone there.

I now have someone sharing the house with me—a friend who has an apartment and found it a real struggle paying it off, so we decided she would move in here and put tenants in the apartment. It's nice. We are very independent. Sometimes we hardly see each other all week, but it's a good feeling knowing that you are not actually alone. You can get awfully lazy about all sorts of things if you don't have someone around. You tend to take shortcuts in the kitchen, for example. You could eat the same pasta for a week if you weren't careful. If we are both here at the same time, we cook and eat together. I wouldn't have just anybody living here, just anybody renting for the sake of it. I don't know whether this is part of getting old or of having my own way for far too long, but I am too jealous of my space to share it with just anyone. I wonder if this is the reason I don't particularly try to find a relationship with a man. Maybe I don't want to share the bathroom.

From a widow's point of view, company is important on a number of levels: sharing ideas, making decisions. I've sometimes felt very lonely making decisions about the children from time to time or trying to advise them without their father. That has been really hard. It would be nice to have someone to make those decisions with or to go on holidays with. I was 40 when Stephen died and, after I crawled out from whatever swamp I had been inhabiting, I wondered for a long time what was going to happen to me. For a couple of years I thought that. There was still a lot of crying to go through. I quite like being solitary from time to time, but being lonely is a totally different thing. The loneliness still creeps up on me occasionally. That's why it's nice having someone to share the house with, because I know at some point they will come home and there will be another human voice and conversation. I've often wondered what is going to happen to me. Where I am going to grow old? Who I am going to grow old with or if it's going to be entirely alone. You can actually get terribly depressed about it if you wake up at 2 o'clock in the morning. I'd like to keep on working, but I suppose there comes a time when you have to stop and I can't imagine that. I'm working very hard on the relationships I do have with a number of close friends because I think they will be very valuable when I finally stop working. I've fortunately got a couple of friends who are a bit younger than me, in their thirties, and their children are quite small. I get a lot of pleasure out of that because I am an honorary aunt.

One of the things I am constantly trying to make decisions about is what to do with my house. At one stage I put in an application to work at a school in Europe. This was through an agency in Australia which interviews people and makes a short video of that interview so that they can liaise with overseas schools. These schools can look at the video to make selections. I had all of this done and I was really interested at one point but I went cold on the idea. I'm not too sure why. I think I wasn't ready to do it or I'd worked out that it was just me trying to construct some sort of change when I didn't necessarily need to change physically.

What I eventually did was leave full-time work at the end of 1994. That was a big step as I'd been with that school for a long time. I'd suddenly decided that I couldn't do that job any more with sufficient enthusiasm. It was time to be doing something different. I wish I was a bit more impetuous. I tend to work things through in a painstaking fashion. So it takes me a long time to change. It would still be fun to live overseas, and maybe it is something I still might go and try. I have a strong emotional tie to the house, but I've got to the point now where I can envisage selling it and moving away from it. For a long time I couldn't have done that. Stephen built the house. He built it for the children and me, despite all the horror of what was going on at the time. It's taken a long time to get through that. It took on a 'relic' significance. I'm beyond that now, although I'd hate to leave the garden. I try to do a fair bit of gardening, although while I was working full-time I had the odd gardener in to pull all the weeds out.

I used to be a regular tennis player and I'd like to play again but my back needs careful handling these days so I tend to go swimming and do yoga. I go to yoga all the time and swim once or twice a week. I hate swimming but it's really good exercise so I consciously go off and swim and I take a friend with me, otherwise I wouldn't do it.

There is another reason why I would consider moving. The suburbs are not the place to live if you think you want to meet someone of the opposite sex, who is available. For that the suburbs generally are not the place to be, particularly this sort of suburb. This is Mr and Mrs Average with 2.5 kids. Everyone is paired. Although if you looked carefully you would see a lot more people like me, living on their own. Something like one in every three households consist of single-parent families, something huge. I don't know whether I'll ever resolve where I'll move to, but eventually this place will have to go. I can't imagine staying here for the rest of my life. I have stayed here for longer that I had intended. It seems to keep happening. Just when my daughter and I got the house valued, decided on which real estate agent to use and looked at various places, I got a job centred in this area, so I thought, it would be ridiculous to move and I stayed.

When the first anniversary of Stephen's death was coming up, it seemed to me to be a terrifying prospect. So I arranged early in the year to take the children to England for Christmas where my sister lives with her family. I felt that I needed to be with family. That's what I did that first year. It had been an awful year. I spent a lot of time in lawyers' offices and a lot of time extracting money from insurance people. I have a vision of that year sitting in a lawyer's office. With regard to finance and money, Stephen was quite an extraordinary person, because he had taken out a lot of insurance as a young person in his early twenties. It was just as well he did. But after his heart problem was diagnosed, he had a couple of opportunities to upgrade the insurance policy that he had, without a medical, so he did. When it came to paying out, the insurance company wanted to know when he had been diagnosed with heart problems. They actually did come up with the money because, as the lawyer said, insurance companies don't like to be held accountable for widows and children, but there was a bit of a fight. That, and getting by, was what I remember of that first year.

So we went to England for the anniversary but it was miserable. It was lovely to be with my sister but it was winter in England and when we arrived there wasn't one green thing to be seen. It was bleak and grotty and cold. It was really very hard that whole six or eight weeks we were away. I had gone with steely determination to take the children to some place different and try to associate Christmas with somewhere else. We were going to see some of England and I was planning to take them to Paris. It was such hard work. The children were lovely, they did their very best, but they hadn't been overseas before and it was cold and they were just so sad as they were missing their father. I sometimes look back and wonder what it was all about. I suppose I think now it was about escaping. I still find the twelfth of December really dreadful, but probably a bit less so. Time certainly is a leveller. Things get into better perspective. The guilt I felt for years is now in better perspective.

I can look back on that and I can say it was awful for Stephen, but it was also awful for me.

I think people look at me as a widow. Divorcees are probably treated slightly differently. Whatever you are, some women consider you a bit of a threat. They think you might want to race off with their husbands. That's the last thing on my mind after my experiences. I certainly noted a change, but it was difficult to put my finger on. You think maybe they never really liked you anyway. It changes things. The relationships I found easiest and most valuable were the ones I'd worked on myself over the past few years and they were the people who really knew how to behave in this situation. Some of them were people I worked with, so we had something in common. They saw me on a day-to-day basis, so perhaps they understood the situation more fully. The friends I've met through that network tend to be people like counsellors who deal with people in their work, rather than particularly active men or housewifely women.

When I was first widowed I only wanted to talk to what I called normal people, not widows. In recent years, though, I have become interested in the experiences of other widows. Widowhood reminds me of someone dressed in black from the eighteenth century so I don't think widow is a very good word. Relationships with other people changed and I found I had to make relationships that were new, or make them again. Being single makes you feel very self-conscious in this society. If you are young, very young, you can get away with it because it might be that you have chosen to be single. But if you are my age, of my generation, then you feel as though you stand out like a sore thumb. I'm always the odd person out at a dinner party. Widowhood for me is associated with the notion of the difficulty of singleness.

HELEN

Helen and Len had been married for more than 55 years when Len died of a misdiagnosed brain tumour at the age of 82. Faced with living the remainder of her life without her husband, Helen, at 77, says there are certainties—independence, friends, financial security and lifelong pleasures such as bridge—which help sustain her and which have gradually reduced the number of days each month she feels unable to cope with the reality that they are no longer together. Helen talks about the elements which are necessary to provide a balanced, long-term relationship, the advantages and disadvantages of living her life in a rural environment and her thoughts about her future. She is a woman who has always held strong individual opinions while sharing the daily decision-making with her husband, a career high school teacher and headmaster. It is her belief that, after 55 years of living with the same person in a happy, balanced relationship, it is equally important after that person's death to get on with living, despite the fact that she says she can never forgive the doctors and hospital that made her husband's last days unbearable.

The months before Len died of a brain tumour were the worst of our lives. He died in January but he had begun to feel unwell four months earlier. He complained of dizziness and headaches, which was unusual for him, because he was so fit and healthy. He had seen his local doctor and been to the local hospital but he finally felt so unwell he was transferred to the larger base hospital, an hour away from home. However, the doctors at the base hospital and his local doctor could find no specific cause for his terrible pain. They said he must have had a mild stroke. He knew himself that wasn't the case, but even after he went into hospital for the second time with acute pain they had the same opinion.

The worst part was that they made him suffer two weeks of rehabilitation for a stroke when all the time the brain tumor was getting worse. They were determined it was a stroke. Poor Len. He wanted them to send him to the city for a specialist check, to make sure they were right, but they kept insisting so we went along with the diagnosis while all the time he was getting progressively worse. I was beside myself with grief. Our daughter, who is a registered nurse, was also distraught because she could see there appeared to be more to his suffering.

Len said—when he came home—that the two weeks he was kept in rehabilitation were the worst two weeks of his life. It was terrible because all the time I thought he should be improving and we were told to do certain things for his condition, but his general state of health deteriorated week by week. If we had known then it was a brain tumour we could have dealt with it. We could have spent our last few months together preparing for it instead of being given false hope that he was going to get better. I will never forgive the doctors for what they did. Never.

When we eventually got him sent off by air ambulance to the city, which was only a few weeks before he died, they did a scan and, sure enough, there was the tumour. I suppose he knew all along it was worse than expected but the tragedy was that he was being treated for something entirely different. A stroke victim has to do exercises, but that was the worst thing for Len. His physical pain in enduring that was absolutely terrible. It was awful to watch him, knowing he was getting worse, rather than getting better.

He was in the local hospital for a couple of weeks before he died. He had a lot of visitors, and he said his farewells to a lot of people during that time. It would have been so much better, though, if he had known earlier, which he could have if the hospital staff had not made a misdiagnosis.

The really awful part was watching a man who had always been a prolific reader, and who had an excellent memory right up until a few months before, get to the stage where he had difficulty speaking and remembering what was happening from day to day.

While he was still at home, his condition deteriorated each week. In the beginning he was using a walking frame to get around and to get into the shower, but within a week or two—from being normal and not needing any assistance to do these things—he was unable to use the frame and had to be supported on both sides to get to the bathroom. I would have done anything to help him of course, but it was awful because he was getting progressively worse when he should have been getting better. I will never forgive the doctors.

The relationship I had with Len, that was the whole core of me. Even as much as a year after he died I didn't know how I was going to cope. Well, I guess I thought, 'I can lie on the ground and kick my heels. But Len's dead. Whatever I do I'm going to become a total bore to everybody or I'm going to pick myself up and make the best of what's left.' And I think that's what Len would have expected me to do. He always said, 'It's no use whipping the cat. You've got to get on.'

I don't know what other people would do. One friend said you never get over it, but you've got to get on with it. You never forget. And I firmly believe you don't have to get over it. That's part of the grieving process. You don't have to ever get over losing your partner and I think it's important for women, especially older women, to realise they can even enter new relationships, but they don't have to abandon everything they had previously to do so. Len always used to say girls should marry men younger than themselves because they live longer. He said if he'd been five years younger than me we probably would have had more chance of not having so long apart.

One of the hardest things to do after Len died was to get out of the house. I'd go around to my daughter's place across town but not much further, especially for the first few weeks. At the time and just after, I didn't particularly want to see anybody, not even good friends I'd had for years, but I now know it's extremely important to do that.

One particular friend I remember. She lives about 70 kilometres out of town and she went to Len's funeral service, but there were so many people there I didn't get to talk to her. She rang me one day soon after and said, 'I'm coming into town to take you to lunch. I didn't send you flowers and I didn't get a chance to speak to you at the service so I'm coming in to take you to lunch.' Well I thought she should just come and have lunch here at my place, but no, she said, 'I'm coming to take you out to lunch.' We went out and then we came back here and had coffee.

That was a couple of months after the funeral. And that was probably the best thing she could have done for me. I didn't want flowers. She was right. That would have only made me feel worse. I now know that I really needed someone to help me get out of my house into the town and to get over my grief by seeing that other people were still going on with their own lives. We take it in turns now, going out and buying lunch. We might only go to the local coffee shop— there aren't too many places in this small town—but it doesn't matter because it's something to look forward to.

I suppose part of the way through the really bleak patches, in the circumstances, is to make sure you keep doing the things you always did and one of those must be grooming. I'm probably a bit vain: I like to be neat, I don't like looking sloppy. I think it's important not to let yourself go. I'm aware of my appearance but I suppose it could become easy not to bother. Sometimes I have to force myself to maintain a standard but I remember Len said when he retired that he was not going to change the way he dressed. 'I'm not going to go down the street looking like a ragbag,' he said. And he was right. You can't let yourself go, even if it is only for your own satisfaction. I just can't bear the look of myself if I'm not dressed properly every day. It's a certain amount of pride probably.

I don't even stay in bed as long as I used to when Len was here. I get up earlier now. I only have an orange juice and a piece of toast for breakfast. I have exactly the same sort of meals for lunch and dinner that I had before, but now I only prepare enough for one. I think it's very important though to keep up that same routine at mealtimes.

And I read a lot. We always used to get into bed at night and read for an hour or more. I still do that and I find television a tremendous boost. In fact, a friend whose husband died several years ago said, 'Thank God for television.' Some people turn it on just to hear a voice in the house. But I use radio for that. I like listening to the radio. I will watch the cricket a lot on television in summer. I switch between the cricket and the golf. Len liked cricket and golf too. I can watch it all day. I suppose a lot of people want their regular daytime shows but, despite television and radio, the loneliness is one of the hardest things to deal with. I still think, 'Oh, I'll tell Len something' and then oh, I remember, yes . . .

I haven't found a need to pray, or to go back to the church in any regular way, since Len died. I was a very good Presbyterian, but when my grand-daughter got leukaemia some years ago I couldn't even pray. I went to Sunday school every Sunday when I was a child, and to church, but when my grand-daughter got sick I really lost any belief in the church. I firmly believe when you're dead, you're dead and that's it. I can't see how it can be any other way.

I know women who have moved out of their family homes, or moved to other towns or to the coast when their husbands die but I'm not sure about the value of making conscious, complete changes. We almost made a decision to move to the coast not long before we came here, but imagine how awful it would be now, with Len gone. I would not know anyone. I had already moved here [out of the family home and into a retirement unit] when Len died. We'd lived very happily here, even though it was for less than three months, but I could never contemplate moving again, not even back in with my daughter and grand-daughter. Never. Even when I'd come down from the hospital after visiting Len all day, I'd open the door and this place would sort of smile at me. It's a very welcoming place. And I don't miss the garden. Not really—you know how some people have a garden and they bury themselves in it, I mean, they can lose themselves in it. Whereas I, it's silly to say it—but if I start cooking, I get lighthearted. I just love cooking. And I love bridge. Nothing that's very productive, I suppose. But I don't think at my age I have to be. I've had my productive years.

Len and I were really good friends and most things we did together. He spent a lot of time in the garden, in his shed, during his retirement but, you see, he could do that. He was more or less sufficient unto himself. We were such good friends, that's why the gap is so tremendous. We used to play golf together when we first came here. I played four days a week—Tuesday and Thursday, and we played twice at the weekends. We had a lovely time, we really did.

He was involved in a lot of community activity too. He was usually out a couple of nights each week when he was working. There was Rotary, Legacy, RSL. Once we came here he was more involved in the headmaster's job, of course. But you know, I couldn't bring myself to go to the Legacy Christmas party the year after he died. Len was such a force in the place. I thought, 'Just at the moment, that's something I can't do.' I thought I may be able to go the next year and I did, but not that first year. It is good to get out and to get involved with things, but some things are just too raw. Maybe they get easier as the years go by.

If I was asked to describe my life I would have to say I was totally fulfilled and happy. A lot of people don't have happy circumstances. I had a good husband. I had no worries—no financial worries. I didn't even pay a bill. I used to just run them up. But by the same token I knew what I could afford. I didn't really want to do any of the financial management. That's why I didn't think I'd be able to manage on my own. There was a five-year age difference between us and I suppose I've been cosseted all my life, really. My mother looked after me til Len took over and I've never had to fend for myself. Even now he's left me totally independent.

I suppose there was a lesson for me with my own mother. When she was older, she said to me she was becoming dependent upon her neighbours and she said she didn't like it because it was not their job to look after her. Just after that she caught the influenza which had killed a dear friend of hers. While she was recovering she came to stay with us, but the old toad wrote and made a booking at a retirement home, back in the city. That was off her own bat. Len had said, while ever he had a home, she had one. She thought that was the nicest thing she'd ever heard. She said, 'Oh no Len. I'll come and stay for a while, but I wouldn't stay long because it would destroy a beautiful friendship.'

There's nothing worse than feeling you're in the way. It's alright while you're active but it's lovely to have somewhere of your very own. When I come home here, this place smiles at me. I wouldn't give that feeling up for anything. I don't want to give up my independence. While ever you can keep your independence, you must do it. I think you want to cling to that. You need to cling to it for your own well-being. I remember a generation or two ago there was often one poor unfortunate daughter who never married because she had to look after mum and dad. A terrible situation. They get bitter. They can't help it. Ruins the whole setup, the whole relationship. Independence is so precious. You need it more as you get older. Once you lose that, you just become a vegetable. Your daughter or son might want you to feel that you're not in the way, but you don't, because the place you live in isn't yours and what's more you haven't got any chance of getting your independence back again.

I went west in 1950. I was 21 when I was married, so I must have been 25, I suppose, when I left the town my mother lived in. I probably wouldn't have thought about getting married when I was 21 except for the war. Len was 25. He went into service in May 1940 and we were married on New Year's eve 1940, the day after he asked me. We had six months together then he was overseas for two years.

It was a horrible thing to consider, that you would get married and then have your husband go off to fight not knowing whether he'd come back or not, but there were a lot of us in the same situation; you just had to make the most of it. I hated the idea of him going away. It might have been ten years for all I knew. It could have been any time. The only saving grace was that he wrote to me regularly. I might get four or five letters together and then none for five weeks. He always used to write, 'I'm going to shave my moustache off' when he looked like coming home, even though he didn't always have a moustache.

When he finally came back after seeing action in Africa and the Middle East we had four years in the same town in which my family lived and then he went west as a high school maths master. When we came here he had a choice. He could have gone to a couple of leading city boys' schools, because by that stage he was pretty high up on the list. He could have had a school up north which would have been closer to our daughter who was doing her nursing training, but neither of us wanted to go to a city. He'd been brought up in the country and we both loved country life. He didn't like one town quite so much, although I still have a lot of friends from there. We were out west for eight years, which doesn't seem long. It seemed a long time then. We were four years in one other town and more than 30 here. We came here in 1962.

I'd never been away from my mother, even after four years of marriage, and she said when it was time to go, 'Well I'm afraid my dear you must go where your husband goes.' I didn't ever not think of it, of course. I wouldn't have contemplated staying with her, but it was just a first reaction I suppose. I wondered how I would get on.

Life wasn't really difficult when we arrived. Not really. It was 1950, I was 30 and our daughter was 5. There was a network of people I met. I became pretty friendly with one particular woman. We met at golf. I started to play golf regularly. I had played quite a bit before I was married. I'd also learned to play bridge when I was younger although there was no bridge playing out west. I started to play with my mother when I had to make up a four occasionally, which I didn't like very much. I was 17 then, I think, and an aunt said, 'Look, when you get old it's the greatest way of entertainment as long as you can hold thirteen cards and you can see.' Bridge has been an absolute saviour to me. I mean I know it's not very productive, but I've reached the stage where I want to do what I want to do. Len wasn't madly keen about the game. We played a bit together before we came here but he wasn't mad about it. Anyway, I used to play regularly with another woman here and then she went away, so Len volunteered to fill in and he really grew to enjoy playing.

I've found that friends are very important now, although they always have been to me. A lot of friends I made in this town 30 years ago, so some have died. When I'm playing bridge I tend to be associating with people who are ten or fifteen years younger. I had a friend in the second town we lived in, and she had a sister-in-law, also Helen, who lives just around the corner from me here. I find the friends Len and I had as joint friends—husbands and wives—are now, like me, widows and widowers. I think living in the country makes a difference to how often you see your remaining friends. It's the proximity, whereas in the city you can be a couple of suburbs away. It makes a difference. You go down the street here and you see them. Even the friends who live out of town you regularly see down the street.

I can remember things better from my childhood than I can remember what happened last week. I went to an eightieth birthday party not long ago and I said something about remembering and another woman said she couldn't remember because she was only a kid, only about ten, and one of the other women said she could remember when she was four. I remember my early life, whereas I have probably already blotted out the time leading up to Len's death.

The reason we came here was so Len could take up a headmaster's position. He retired when he was 59. He'd been pretty nervy and he said to me, 'The job's worrying me quite a lot and it used not to.' It was almost the September holidays and he said, 'I don't think I can go to work tomorrow. I'll ring the district inspector. I'm not well.'

The district inspector came down and asked how much sick leave he'd had over the years. Len said eleven days in 30-odd years so the district inspector said we should go away for a while. Len said he had some reports he had to finish and get signed. The district inspector took them from Len, put them under his arm and said, 'We'll give those to the deputy.' There were a lot of reasons for it.

I was 41 when we came here and Len was 46. We didn't contemplate retiring here. We didn't think about retiring then, you see. After we'd been here a few years we just loved it—the town and the people. We had the headmaster's house for four years and after four years you're supposed to look for something else. They don't throw you out on the street but they suggest it's a good thing if you do something about it. So he said, 'If we build a house here, I think perhaps we could decide to stay and retire here. We've both seen people who've dashed off to the coast in retirement and been as lonely as billyo. When one of them dies you're left in a strange place.'

I'm quite convinced the older you get the more difficult it is to settle in. You can't be bothered. People got on very well before you came and they'll get on very well after you've left. You're the one who has to make the effort. I mean their lives go on whether you're there or you're not. We decided we didn't have the energy to begin again and be as happy as we were. Really, if you're happy being somewhere, why move?

Throughout his career he'd tell me things that worried him or amused him, or pleased him. I really think he had a nice little group of blokes—the manager of the bank, the newspaper owner, and a couple of property owners and they had a little clique at the RSL club. Each afternoon they'd go down just for an hour or so.

By this stage our daughter Bronnie had left home and she was working. She left and went off to do her nursing. We started going off to the far north coast when Len got sick and retired. We went up the coast and stayed at motels for three weeks or so and when we came back he said, 'I'd like to go away for two or three months.' I said that sounded like a good idea. He said motelling becomes a bit expensive after two or three months and asked me how I would feel about staying in a caravan. Well I'd have gone in a dray to get him better. He asked me if I was sure about it and I said I was quite happy. Someone said there was a caravan for sale down the road and it had only had one trip so we went down and had a look at it. We knew nothing about it, we just bought it. He took it out to where the wheat stacks were—a big cement patch out near the pits—and he did a few backs and forwards and turns and said, 'Oh, I think I can manage it.' We threw our gear in and off we went.

We were away for three months. We didn't plan to be away that long until we got there. We stayed at all the resorts on the way up and the only thing he did without me was fishing—I couldn't stand it.

In 1940, coming down from Darwin, they had gone into Bowen to get some coal for the boat and I had a wire from Len to say he was at Bowen and would be home soon. They had a wonderful time there, he said. They had a day on the booze, you see, and there was this long pier and several of them went into the water. So he said he would like to go and have a look at Bowen again. It was just magnificent. The weather was superb. There was a beautiful sandy bottom on Horseshoe Bay. But we went on and we said while we're here we better go to Cairns. We went up to the Atherton Tablelands and back in to Cairns. Len said, 'I don't like this as much as Bowen, do you?' and I said I didn't, so we decided to go back to Bowen. We stayed a month. And we went back each year until my grand-daughter Penny got leukaemia. We missed five years then. Before that, we would leave around late May or early June and come back in September.

I'd never go back up there now though. Never. I couldn't bear it. I was talking to a friend down south—we correspond, simply because our husbands died about three months apart—and she said she wouldn't go back to the same holiday places they went to either. Too many memories.

I haven't really thought about taking holidays at this stage. Not at the moment. I'm going to Hobart in February for a while, though, but I just want to get myself settled here. I don't feel I want to go away.

The fact that I have no money worries has helped me a great deal. Len left me very comfortably off. I also get a war veterans' pension and it's not taxable nor is it means tested. I could live on that and all the other superannuation just accrues. There is also a small parcel of shares Len was left by his mother. When his mother died, his brother Frank was executor and Frank said what about the shares? Len said sell them. Anyway, Frank got fed up with trying to organise them and said to his brothers and sister you can all have them and do what you like with them. Len started to get interested straight away. He'd read the papers and say we lost some money this week. And I'd say what's it matter if you don't propose to sell them? I don't look at the papers to check the shares. With the retirement account I have at the bank I can get 7 per cent so each time something matures I just let it go in there.

Len always had a secure job with the education department so we were never really worried about our financial security. He thought about changing once. The local accountant wanted him to go into partnership with him but Len said, 'Not on your life. For one thing, you and I would fall out in ten minutes, and for another thing why should I start something else when my future and my wife's future is totally secure?'

Life is a lot different now. People change jobs more frequently. Which is probably a good thing in lots of ways. You can get very lazy if your job's just there. Although Len would never have taken security over the enjoyment of work.

Because I have financial security, because I've got that behind me, there may be things that I will want to do in the next ten or fifteen years but I haven't thought of them yet. I don't know. If I did take on something new it would have to interest me greatly and I don't know, if it involved much effort I don't think I could be bothered. I'm pretty lazy. Always have been. I don't think I've ever lived up to my potential because I've drifted. I'm happy with what I'm doing, I've looked after Len. It was really a labour of love. I just adored him.

My mother was 87 when she died. So theoretically I could live for another ten or fifteen years because I'm in similar health. I don't mind living while I'm active and I can look after myself. I'm a bit of a believer in euthanasia. I think you have to be aware of what you're doing. Len wasn't mentally affected. He went quickly, though. Had he continued like he was for any length of time, I'm quite sure he'd have wanted to use that law.

I've already had someone interested in coming into my life since Len died. They used to go up north to the same holiday spot as us and Janet died just before Len. Her husband rang me—he lives in the next town, 40 minutes away—and said how about coming up and spending the night? This was after Len hadn't been dead more than two months. I said I beg your pardon, Hector? Hector was 80-something. Anyway he said 'You won't?' and I said 'I most certainly won't'. He rang me again and said he wanted to have a very serious talk with me. He was going to the city and would call in on the way back. I thought oh God, what's he going to say? so I said to a neighbour how about coming in, Hec's going to call in on the way back from the city. She said, why? I said, 'Oh he's being silly.' Well, he came in and he said, 'I can't go to Bowen any more.' I said 'You wouldn't want to, would you' and he said, 'Oh well, I just can't anyway. I can't drive that far again.' But, he said, 'I've booked at the Gold Coast and I want you to come.' Well, I said you can want till you're blue in the face Hec, not on your life. I said I'm still grieving for Len, I don't know about you. He'd been married twice, you see. He said if he hadn't married his second wife he'd have had a miserable life. But he was probably only 60 when he remarried. I told him again I was still grieving for Len and he said, 'Oh, are you sure you won't come?' I said I was absolutely certain and I didn't want to hear another word about it. I think men probably think differently about their relationships. Hec must have. Probably all he wanted was a companion, but he wasn't getting me. I couldn't believe it. I used to like him, you know, but he put me right off. After that he asked me how long I was going to be grieving. 'When will you get over it?', he asked. I said this year, next year, sometime . . . 'most likely never Hec'. Anyway he died. He had a fall. It must seem funny, but I went to his funeral. He's out of my life without even having been in it.

Len's and my relationship was all ups, there were no downs. My daughter said to me one day, 'You know Mum, I don't think I ever heard you and Dad raise your voices at each other.' I said we had our disagreements but he never raised his voice. We had disagreements, otherwise we wouldn't be human.

I don't think I would want to move back in with my daughter when I get too old to look after myself. No. I would go to the progressive retirement unit. I would never inflict myself on her. She might think she wants me to for the moment, but I would never do it. I think it's more important to be near enough to enjoy each other's company but be able to go when you need to. The other thing is that Bronnie and I are too much alike really. We get on well, but Bronnie's untidy and I'm tidy you see and I can't take that.

I suppose I'm also very lucky in living here in this unit. Len and I bought it only a short time ago. A certain amount is taken out every year then we get back the remainder. When it gets to a certain point it stops and the remainder goes into my estate. When I'm no longer here, when I'm in the next stage which is a care unit this reverts to the trust.

It's wonderful here because at my age I don't have any worries at all. The fence, for instance, along the side—when it blew down in a storm it was nothing to do with me. The maintenance people just came in and fixed it. If the lights go bung, or the washing machine, someone comes in and fixes it. That's what Len wanted. If I were still living in a house I'd have the responsibility of seeing to the lawn and all those other things. Here I don't have any of that worry and I think that's probably why I feel as good as I feel. I mean I have days when I feel absolutely bloody awful, but each month that goes past I probably have less days when I could just throw in the sponge. There are not many of my direct family members left now. I'm not sure what I would do if I received an extended invitation, say from my brother to come and stay in the city. You see I've lived in the country all my adult life. I don't know that I want to go anywhere for a couple of months.

HISAKO

Hisako was a talented Japanese music student who fell in love with, and eventually married, an Australian much older than her. She had two children, the first conceived before she and Albert were married, which threw her traditional Japanese upbringing into chaos. Her family in Japan refused to journey to Australia for the wedding, virtually cutting off all contact with her. For fifteen years, however, she had what she describes as a wonderful relationship. When Albert was diagnosed with prostate cancer, Hisako felt she would be unable to cope with the grief, the thought of her husband dying and the emptiness she would experience if he did.

Ultimately, after two months in hospital, Albert succumbed to the cancer. Hisako was at his bedside when he died and stayed with him for many hours afterwards. She felt the need to touch every part of his body, to prepare him for the after-life she knew he would be entering and to cope with her grief in the knowledge she would see him again and that his presence would be with her when she returned home to her two primary school-aged children.

When we spoke, Hisako had been widowed for a little more than eighteen months, although she does not picture herself as a widow. She has had to increase her working hours to be able to adequately care for her children and to learn how to cope with making decisions on the day-to-day issues which affect three people. It is her belief that her husband is still with her in spirit. Hisako talked about the way she handled her grief, her thoughts for the future and for her children and the problems she faces as a Japanese woman in a traditionally European culture. Hisako described how she felt the need to deal with her grief personally, with her children and with a few close friends.

Albert was sick for some time before he died. He had been diagnosed with prostate cancer a year earlier. He was in a lot of pain for months beforehand. On the day he died, I had left the children with a neighbour and I went to be with him at the hospital. I was with him all day. He was in pain and he could not speak by this stage. He died at about midnight. I was sitting in a chair beside his bed, watching him. He became very still. I just sat very still and cried and cried. The nursing sister came in and asked me to wait outside as they had things to do to him. After a short time they told me that I could go in and see him, before he started to go stiff. So I went in. I felt so cold. It was not the temperature in the room so much because it was summer. I just felt cold all through. The room he was in had been tidied up by the time I went back in and there was only one spotlight on him and he was all white. He had been bandaged up. He was still warm and—I know this may sound strange—I just wanted to check every part of him. I just wanted to touch his hands. They were still warm. I just cried and cried. I stayed with him for a long time there in that cold room. After a couple of hours I left the hospital and went home to my children. Albert was very much older than me. I was 45 and the children were 12 and 9. He was 65 when he died.

When I came home from the hospital, there was nothing. It was just nothing, empty. I just cried and cried. Because he was diagnosed with prostate cancer some time before he died, I had a time to prepare myself, which made a difference. If you had a husband who died in a car crash or any sudden happening, how could you prepare yourself? In my case, that preparation was very important. I think I started grieving the moment he went into hospital, two months before he died. He was actually in hospital for two months and I would visit him every day. At that time I simply wanted to be with him as long as possible. I prayed that he would come home, but I think deep down I knew he would not be coming back. Not back to the house as he had been. It is very hard to describe the grief that one feels when a loved one, especially a husband, is dying. Prayer was very important to me during that period. I prayed a lot. Albert was suffering a cancer that is very painful and he was in a great deal of pain. In the end, he actually wanted to go. The really horrible part is that I wanted to see him alive as long as possible. When eventually he said, let me go, please let me go, I think my real grief started from there. It has taken eighteen months for me to get over that real, aching grief that I had every day in the beginning. I think I am better able to handle everyday things now. I think time has a lot to do with how you feel. I don't think I could have talked about any of this after a short time, not even after a year. It has taken a year and a half for me to be able to come to terms with all sorts of things. I get better and better at handling things as I go along, but I still think about him every day and I always cry.

Albert had been married before he met me but his wife had left him and they were divorced. He had lived in this house with her but she moved out when they were divorced. He lived here for five years alone before we met. I had not been married before I met him. I was born in Japan. I travelled to Australia as a student to study music at the Sydney Conservatorium. I had been to Australia many times before I decided to study here full time. I made the decision to come and study here because I could also use the opportunity to learn English. I had planned to return to Japan after I had finished my full-time studies but after I met Albert, I didn't go back. He was almost 50 when we first met. I was 30. He had children from his first marriage who are around the same age as me. I don't know much about his first marriage, but according to his children from that marriage, Albert was actually quite strict with them. Of course, I don't really know but I think they were closer to their mother. I talked to her after Albert passed away. She went to the funeral and afterwards we sorted out some possessions and other things that went to his sons. We don't have what I would call any sort of relationship. She divorced him and he changed his life after that.

When I met Albert, he was still working. He had been thinking about retirement and eventually he did retire when our first child was born. He said that he would be able to help me around the house and let me pursue my musical interests. I had been teaching music until the baby was born and then I stopped everything and both of us were just absorbed in our baby. I didn't work for quite some time then. I cancelled everybody, all my students—I teach piano—and when I was emotionally ready I started again. Of course, some had found other teachers, but many were waiting for me to start again. Some asked me to start again. Some time after my son was born, I began teaching again and when my daughter was born—that was the second child—I knew better what I was doing. She was born at the end of November so I was able to have a longer holiday and combine it with the Christmas holidays. I started teaching the next February. Thanks to Albert, my financial position is reasonably good. I do have to deal with finances differently now and I have increased the number of hours I teach. I will need to keep doing that and I think I am probably very lucky. But I am in a secure position. In the eighteen months since Albert died I've felt very differently about birthdays and special occasions that we used to share. On Father's Day and his birthday we go to the crematorium. Also, his ashes are in our local Anglican church. We always go to church and when we are there we touch 'Daddy's' plaque. The children talk the same way about him as they would if he were still here. We always talk about 'Daddy': if 'Daddy' were still here, he would think of things the same way as me. He is always watching. That is what I truly always believe. He has been helping us. I asked him when he was in hospital if he would be watching us kindly as usual and, though he couldn't talk, he did try to answer. He could hear and he understood what I said. So I believe he is doing it. When I have a problem, I always pray that Albert and the priest will help us.

Without Albert, I am now a sole parent so I have all the responsibilities of both parents for my children. I think I went through a huge change to overcome that and in my case, because I was brought up in a traditional Japanese culture, I have to adapt to all sorts of other problems that arise. The discipline and the way of bringing up children I think are the same, however. But from the other side—how the children themselves see the situation—I think that in a two-parent family the mother and father have different ideas which come together to deal well with issues, and find the best solutions to all sorts of problems. In my case the children will be a bit biased because they listen to only my ideas.

Sometimes I would like to be able to hear, if Albert were here, what he would think about a particular problem. How would he advise them? It is really very hard to know how they are affected by this, especially such a short time after their father's death but I hope they understand that I try to give them both sides. I just try to talk to them both as if their father were still around and still providing another side to an argument. When Albert died, even though my children were relatively young, they were—and still have been—really very helpful. After he passed away, I said to them 'Dad is gone so we need to help each other.' We cooperate all together. Our pattern changed as I had to get up earlier to get the children off to school. Albert had been retired for some years and I had him with me to help with the children. He was very involved with them and the things they did. He taught scripture at the local primary school because he enjoyed being with children so much. I would say he was a fairly religious man anyway.

A few months after he died, I thought about moving house but then I thought, no way, why should we? Part of my decision to move was based around the garden. Because of the garden—at the moment there is a very nice garden—I didn't think I could take care of everything by myself. Albert had taken care of maintaining the house and he worked very hard in the garden. After he died it became too much of a burden because of the garden and I suppose there are memories of him in the garden so for a short time I thought I would be better off without it. For a few months I wanted a smaller house and small garden which I could look after all myself and get a man in for all the house maintenance. Then suddenly I thought, 'Oh no, I don't want to do it.' I suppose that was eight or nine months or so after he had died. All of a sudden I couldn't imagine the idea of not being in this house.

One of the major problems in my life is that I do not have a good relationship with my own parents, who live in Japan. Since Albert's death, I've promised myself that within two years I would take the children away for a break, so they can understand that they will have lives to get on with. But the idea of going to Japan is not a very good one. If I'd had a good relationship with my family, I would have gone to Japan last year some time. It would also be difficult for me to go on holidays to the places I went with Albert. We didn't take regular holidays, just a few days here and there and the occasional two weeks. I don't think I'd go back, as we have nice memories of those places and I don't want to go without Albert, so I would just leave it that way, as memories. There are just the three of us now and we will go a different way and make new, nice memories.

When someone dies, you miss them being part of your life. You miss them being there every day. I think I miss everything of Albert. Everything he did. But mostly I miss his jokes. He was able to joke about things even right up until when he died. Even when he was in pain he was still able to joke about things. The really difficult part is that I now have to do everything alone. We did all sorts of things together. Everything. Because of the age difference we had different friends but we all got on well. He had friends he had had for a long time who were older and I had my friends and we all mixed and we got on very well. Now that he is dead I don't see a lot of his old friends because they are spread around the country. There is one good friend he had for many years who lives just down the street. He comes here regularly. He still calls in to see that we are OK, but he is also not young, so he has to look after himself.

Albert and I met at a concert. We had a mutual love of music. We would sometimes go to a Japanese restaurant or watch a Japanese movie together. We had many common interests. Albert didn't play but he had a very good ear. He could even criticise my piano playing. He always listened, of course. Early in our relationship we attended many classical concerts and he would compare me with those. We knew each other before we went out, for a few years, then we went out together for just over a year before our son was born. We went to concerts and dinner and movies. We had a nice time getting to know each other. He had been divorced for about five years when we started going out, so he was not simply getting over someone else. He was quite happy by himself but I think, because he was older, he may have been quite lonely.

Because we had a mixed race relationship, there were outside influences that I feel were different to a marriage of one race—two Australians being married or two Japanese. I'm quite easy-going, so I don't think it affected me in the early years. At the time no, I don't think I was affected, but now I think differently and I would say that I would be. I think about it more now. At the time I didn't care. If I had to describe my marriage, I would have to say it was wonderful. I mean, we had a nice relationship. If he had not had cancer he would be still here. He was very fit. He always looked after his health. He had a good diet and he played sports—tennis, golf and he did lots of walking. I think it is really important, to get out and play tennis, to keep busy and not think too much about the actual process of him dying. I try to meet my friends as much as possible. Just to go to lunch together or play tennis. I feel that is a big help. But I will do my routine work first. Do all the house chores first and then I'll have spare time and then I'll take some time off.

I suppose I don't really think of myself as a widow. Actually no, I don't think of myself as that at all, but I am. I am keeping very busy so I can't have time to think of myself as anything, really. I don't ever just sit around and think of myself as a widow. No, never, because I feel that Albert is in here, in this house with me. That is why I don't feel like a widow. Besides, I have to look after the future of my children. That's my task. My future is also to look after my grandchildren. I'm looking forward to seeing them. My son, who is still only in high school, said that will only happen if he marries, and I say, please do. I say you want to marry, don't you?, and he says yes. It would be nice to have lots of family around me, especially at Christmas time. Christmas last year was very sad so I look towards future years. It was just before Christmas that Albert died. Sometimes the children talk about the possibility of them living in Japan in the future. They say that they would like to but they have seen only the good parts of Japan. You can't live there like you can here. There is a very different culture and the cost of living is far higher. I would not advise them to do so. Perhaps for only one year later on they could go, but not now.

Since Albert passed away, the children haven't changed their pattern of doing things although I think they probably will later on when they become teenagers. As a single parent, I am not sure how I will deal with having a boy and a girl who are growing up and will be teenagers. I am not sure what sort of problems they will face and how I will be able to help them respond. In our everyday conversation I reinforce in them little disciplines as much as I can. For instance, I might say about something on the TV, 'That is not good, she was not doing the right thing, she should have done it this way.' They say, 'Yes, of course.' So hopefully, hopefully, my children will be alright in handling their teenage problems.

I don't believe that the children get any support at school with regard to their father dying. I don't think they do anything special to assist them. Actually, they have changed their schools recently so they have both had changes. At the new schools they don't know about Albert at all. Probably my son will feel a difference now as he will have to get up a lot earlier to travel and I also will have to get up early. We were only getting up at about 7 o'clock, but that will change. On weekends, Saturday, we get up and go to sport— my son plays tennis. Sunday we don't get up until 10 o'clock sometimes.

I think people tend not to say anything to the children or to me, because if people say to you, 'I'm sorry about Albert', you feel bad, so it's better not to talk about it at all. I would rather we just dealt with our grief personally, as a family. I don't think people know how to deal with another's grief, with a loss, especially of one so close. People seem to change the way they respond to you. They go out of their way to contact me more than usual, but because of this I am broadening my circle of friendship and that is wonderful. I don't think this would have happened if Albert were still here. We would have kept doing the same as we always did, doing so much together. We would have had a smaller circle of friends. Just our regular friends. I don't think I have changed personally during the past eighteen months. I've always been like this, thinking always of the future. I know that he has passed on, but life must go on and if I was always sad and miserable the children would feel the same way, and that's not good. So I've got to cheer up myself. I'm that sort of a person anyway. Albert was like that too. He was a very positive person. The children too. Every child has a promising future. I get down and I feel sad, but I always think about how I can solve this problem or that problem. I do it that way and always I cheer myself up and I try to get a better result.

I didn't ever think about contacting a widows' society or any other help group after Albert died. I never wanted to do anything like that, never. Friends and neighbours were the most important things in my grieving process, helping me get through it. Without them, things would be very different. Because I married Albert, I haven't had any contact with my family and you need someone to just talk to about your problems. I think everybody needs close friends. My family in Japan, my mother and father and sister broke off all relations with me when I stayed here. When I married

Albert my mother was very distressed. She was upset that I was not marrying a Japanese man and also that I was marrying someone far older than me. It has been very hard for me in this regard because there were people here who also said I was marrying Albert only for security, that I didn't love him and that was the most cruel part. I don't know how people can say things like that.

My childhood, growing up in Japan, was a bit like my son's. I think we are very similar. I learned piano and up until high school I went to a normal school and then went to a school that was musically based. I then went on to university. I went to the music school. Music has always played a major part in my life. I was not involved in performance. I was involved in teaching. I thought a lot about getting married and having a family—a lot like my daughter thinks now: she wants to be a mother. If you ask her what she wants to become, she says she only wants to become a mother. That's what I thought I always wanted: to have a happy family, two children or three. Then I also always wanted to teach the piano. I'm not that good anyway, as a soloist, and teaching is what I wanted to do from childhood. So I have fulfilled those ambitions.

It's hard to say what will happen in the future, but right now, eighteen months later, I feel that I can talk about all this. If you had asked me last year, no. I wasn't ready to talk about it. Even now, as you can see, I cry. I just truly couldn't have talked about any of it earlier. Last year I couldn't have. But now I can. After one year—I can't explain it very well, but I just felt, I'm OK. Not totally, not all the time, I suppose, but compared with last year I'm OK to talk about this. I'm now happy to talk about it because Albert and I had a nice relationship and I find I can talk about that, express how I felt about our relationship even though it makes me very sad. If people all over the world who read your book feel that we had a nice relationship, that is wonderful. If it helps other women in their grieving process then that can only be good. Albert would have wanted me to share my thoughts on this so that it could help other women to understand that, even though the grieving, in the beginning, is almost too hard to bear—no matter what age you are or how long you have had your relationship—and even though it does not get any easier to bear knowing that your husband is not there every day to be part of your life, time does make a difference. A year is an important milestone. Then, after eighteen months, it is easier again. I think after two years and then five it will be easier to understand and talk about even more. But unfortunately Albert had to go.

I have talked about how I coped with the major trauma, the grieving and about my children, about religion, friends, coping with everyday life but what I have not mentioned is the difficulty I experienced with little things, minor things that I took for granted when Albert was around. Like fixing the car. I was truly afraid of what would happen to the car. I did not know anything about the car. As soon as Albert had passed on, I had many problems with the car. Well, what can you do? You have to take it to the garage, don't you, so that was what I did. The local service mechanic knew Albert very well. But I decided I would study about the car. Now I know about the car, more than I did before, and I check it. Now there is maintenance I can do. I have to ask someone to come in and do other jobs around the house, like mending guttering and other things that I don't have tools for. My son mows the lawn and I do the weeding and we share the jobs. Also, one of my friends is a handyman and he offered to do any jobs that I needed. I am so happy to know him and his family and he always comes when I have a problem. He always comes and fixes things. He did the gutters. Sometimes he charges a little and sometimes it is free and that is truly great.

One of the things I have not been regular with lately, however, is going to church. I have not been and I feel so bad about it. We used to go on Sunday regularly at 10 o'clock, but as I said, Sunday is the only morning we can sleep in. So we now go to night service sometimes on a Thursday at 8 o'clock and Easter and Christmas and other special occasions. No one from the church came to offer assistance after Albert died and I would not have expected them to, even though we have always been involved in the church. Unless you go and ask them for assistance they don't approach you in your home.

Last year, for months after Albert's death, when a problem came I solved it somehow. I can't remember how, but I just did it. I just did it because I had to. This year I have more time to think and I am putting things in the calendar so I know when all the bills are due and I can plan. I put in what I have to do about the car so when it goes to have a regular service I can predict what is happening. Some things do come up unexpectedly and I can't plan for those, but I think I keep track quite well.

We will stay here in this house as long as possible. We have no reason to make that sort of change now. We are within walking distance of the railway station and it's very convenient to everything. I don't know what the future holds for me and the children with regard to having other people in our lives. Anything can be possible. I can just say that I don't know. I will see what happens. But if there was someone nice that I could love, then maybe I might. The neighbours say that we are all widows now, a row of us in the street. They say that at the moment I am busy with the children but when the children leave me, I will be very lonely. I will need someone. This is what they have said many times. If you see someone nice, or have a chance like that, well—why not? Last year I said, no, no never, but now I say, why not, maybe. I'll see what happens. I'm nearly 47.

When I thought about what I could tell you about how I felt when he first died, it was simply that I felt I wanted to be with him. No thinking. It was just what I wanted. That was all. I know that may sound irrational because I have children to look after, but that was my first reaction. I wanted to go with him. A lot of women, especially older ones, have said different things about how they have coped with the grieving, especially the time immediately after the death of their husbands, but mostly they have said something to their husbands immediately before they died, those who had the opportunity. Then they said they had just gone on with the funeral arrangements and what they had to do.

Albert's funeral was arranged by the rector because I was crying all the time and I could not talk on the phone. The children both went to the funeral. Whenever I cried, they cried, so I had to try to stop but I couldn't, I just couldn't. Many of Albert's friends from his earlier life came to the funeral too, along with neighbours and friends. One neighbour commented to me that it was a very sad funeral. I said, 'Was there ever any happy funeral?' The Christian funeral ceremony is very similar in Japan to Australia, but Albert and I had not talked about the possibility of his dying, even when he was diagnosed with the prostate cancer, so we had not arranged anything specific. He had left a will with his wishes for cremation and other instructions to be carried out. When I go, I will do the same thing as Albert and be cremated. Actually, I am looking forward to seeing him again.

JENNY

Jenny was widowed at 25. Her husband, John, had died from cancer and she was left with three children all under the age of 8. For two years before his death, Jenny watched her husband undergo massive chemotherapy treatment, saw his thriving business fall apart then stood by him as he suffered a painful and prolonged death. Now, seven years later, at 33, she is still learning to live with her loss, trying to make ends meet as she puts her children through school and provides a home and a life for them and herself, despite the heavy financial burden and the unavailability of any social support mechanisms other than family and friends.

When I had death at my doorstep, when my husband had been diagnosed with cancer, I was 25 and I thought I was old and mature. Now, seven years later, I see my younger brothers and sisters at that age and I just feel so old. I felt that being a widow was only something that should happen to you when you were 50 or older. There was a real sense of disbelief. I think I was so young for that to happen to my husband and to happen to me and to my kids.

In the seven years since John died there hasn't really been one big dramatic change in my life. It was very, very hard for the children for the first two years. At the start we would go regularly to the cemetery—Father's Day, birthday and other days in between. I found myself thinking, gee, it's been two or three years and I was still a mess. I would leave the cemetery crying, even after that length of time. Then one day I realised I had just walked out of the gate and I felt OK. I was more concerned then about feeling guilty. I had been there, and gone away without being so emotional. Time is an absolutely amazing thing. Right after John died, people told me time would make a difference. I got sick of hearing that, but it does. I still get emotional at certain times.

I have filled the gap by doing different courses, studying and work, motherhood and everything else. Just being a single mother is so demanding. And working and trying to study. I am very, very busy and I like to be busy. If I wasn't, I think I would be a mess. Right from day one I had to be busy to handle the whole situation.

I think as a single parent I now handle my children differently. In a two-parent family you can negotiate, you can give in, but as a solo parent when you say no, you've got to mean no. And you've got to be aware of different things. I find myself going fishing—I've got to play that fatherly role as well, because even when people are divorced the children can still go to the father. As a single parent I have to take on both. I do a lot more because of that.

I suppose I do get a bit annoyed, and a bit sensitive, that people classify me as a single mother or widow. One of the things that really breaks my heart is when the school produces a list and it has the surname and the class and mother's and father's name on it. On my daughter's it has her name and mine and then in brackets for father it has 'deceased'. Because I'm widowed, people tend to treat me differently from the other single mothers. There is a real social issue about single mothers but people seem to think widows are different. There have been other little things that really annoy me such as receiving mail addressed to Ms. I'm still Mrs and I always will be and I don't know why people want to try to alter that fact. I still wear my wedding ring. That was a funny issue—should I or shouldn't I wear it when I was going out? I thought, damn it, I'm not ashamed of it.

One interesting thing about being a widow and being so young is that I had a good sexual relationship with John and now, of course, that is gone. I have not been involved in many relationships since his death, especially sexual ones, and that is because I am exhausted by the end of each day just dealing with everything that I have to deal with, having three children. Otherwise, I might be at the local clubs meeting people.

I'm not out there looking for anyone, although recently there was an incident which made me think. I had been visiting a friend who had had a baby. My youngest son was with me and he said, after buying a present for the baby, what a beautiful baby girl she was and he wished he had a baby sister. I explained that I could not do that because I was no longer married. He asked when he was going to get another dad. We were standing in a carpark and I just cried. I said something like one day, maybe if I got to find someone who I really, really loved. That set me thinking about all sorts of other situations and sending me into some sort of guilt because I was depriving my children of a father while being preoccupied with myself. I decided that when I met some-one I would meet them at the right time, but I did wonder if I had been depriving my children. My youngest has said the same thing again during the past few years and I have a different attitude to it now. I realised that, while I was happy doing all the things I was doing to take up the space, maybe I had to think more about how they felt.

I don't want to work nine to five, five days a week while my children grow up. I would like to have the qualifications to work three days a week so I can be with them at all the things they need me for. After seven years, I still get into ruts, but I couldn't see myself going into a long-term depres-sion. I feel as if I have aged since John died and it's interesting how people perceive his death. People generally don't know how to deal with it when I tell them. They feel very uncomfortable. They relate it to someone they know who has died. It is interesting to watch how other people deal with their own grief through me. I tend to listen a lot when people want to tell me about their own death experiences. When I hear of other people who have cancer I find them easier to relate to, with their circumstances, and I probably put more into them than I would into others.

After John passed away, I would sometimes go to the doctor and he would ask me questions about my youngest boy. I would say, don't ask me questions about anything to do with the past two years: I can't remember. I'd think, when someone asked me something, why don't I know that? I have a very good memory. When it came to dates, I had so much on my plate, it was incredible. As far as the grieving process goes, I think I started the day they diagnosed the cancer. For two years prior to John passing away there was a certain amount of grief that I went through. But at the time of the death it was tenfold.

John was a big man. He was six foot tall. He was very fit. He liked a beer, but he didn't smoke. The family doctor knew him only from taking the children to be immunised. He had never been to the doctor. It all started when he caught the flu. He couldn't seem to shake it off. We were living in the south-west. We had a very successful transport business and we had bought one other similar business a few months earlier. We had a team of drivers. Even with the flu and chest infection, John would get up and go to work and I remember arguing with him and saying that he needed to see a doctor and get something done about it. He was running himself into the ground.

He was diagnosed with cancer when our youngest was barely two months old. One Sunday, John just collapsed in the bathroom. He went giddy and lost his balance. I made him go straight to the local medical centre and they said he had pneumonia. They put him on antibiotics and the next day, Monday, he went back in the late afternoon. He came home—I was changing the baby's nappy in the loungeroom in front of the heater—it was a bleak, wet winter day. He just came in and sat on the lounge, threw the x-rays down and said, out of the blue, that they thought he may have cancer. I said I didn't think that was very funny.

I picked up the x-rays, then I picked up the telephone and rang our family doctor. I told him John had collapsed and some x-rays had been taken. That was Monday night at 6 o'clock. He calmed me down and asked who we had been referred to. He said he knew him very well and asked when the appointment was. When I said it was for the next day he seemed more concerned. The next day we went to a radiology centre. At this stage we hadn't told anyone, not family nor friends. We decided to wait until we found out more. We were both very worried. When we were at home— between going to the specialists—we were really optimistic. We kept saying it would be something else. But that was just me psyching him up.

We went to a specialist who sat us down and asked us a lot of questions. John was giving him answers—answers that I knew nothing about. He was saying he had night sweats and had lost weight. I had been oblivious. It just all happened. I'd noticed he had lost a bit of weight but I thought it was because he was eating healthier foods instead of junk. I was outraged. I was his wife. I slept with him. I could not understand how this could have happened without me knowing. The specialist was very concerned. He told us to rush downstairs to the radiology department to have immediate testing. It was 5 o'clock in the afternoon. They would normally have closed their doors by this time but they were told to stay open. John broke down then. He was in tears, holding on to me as we walked half a block from the surgery to the main part of the hospital.

I had organised with a neighbour to collect the children from preschool. I had told her we had a bit of a scare and asked if she would mind picking them up. I ended up in tears at the radiology centre. It was all so difficult. I rang my sister and burst into tears. I told her the whole story. By the time we got home, she'd raced from her place to be there and that's when everything started. John was booked into hospital. We got the results of the biopsy the next day which showed the cancer was malignant. From there he had a course of chemotherapy for three months. We would go to the hospital every second week. It knocked him around terribly. As soon as that needle would go into him he would get nauseous. It was terrible. He ended up hating Tuesdays.

We had a lot of work at that stage and the people working for us tried to keep going. We kept the business going because we thought he was going to get better. We were told that, out of all the cancers, the one he had was the 'luckiest' because it has a very, very high success rate. The doctors all said that—while the diagnosis wasn't good—with his physique and medical history it should be OK. But the chemotherapy knocked him around terribly. He was very, very sick. He would be knocked out for a day or two after each treatment. It was bad.

We had a lot of problems at this stage, besides the cancer. We had a contractor who owed us money who basically told me to go jump because John would be dead in six months anyway. All of a sudden, without him being on the road, we had a lot of problems. We seemed to be working to alleviate all forms of stress on him. When he was feeling complete and wonderful I would just cook and feed him and feel healthy and happy. He found it hard. He was always asking why it was happening to him. He found it very hard emotionally. Because of that I was the one falsifying things, saying everything would be OK. He was experiencing a lot of anger by this stage. He was angry that it had happened to him. He got angry over the disease and what it had done to him. He got angry over the business side of life and other worries because he couldn't be doing the things he wanted to do. He was so aware that it just wasn't going away. His way of handling the anger was to storm around the house yelling. A lot of the anti-nausea medication he was taking had a depressing side and the pressure was bad enough without that. A couple of years before he was diagnosed he had had an experience with yoga—for relaxation—and he loved it. So he took that up again. The difference—physically, emotionally, mentally—was incredible. He also got involved in alternative medicine. Certain gurus believed that he could heal himself. We went through a lot of that, as people do in times of desperation.

I was brought up in a religious family. We went to church every Sunday as children. I went back to church every Sunday after John was diagnosed. All of a sudden I thought I needed help—help to get from one week to another. I had to have that belief. From that initial meeting, the parish priest would come and visit. John was christened but he wasn't a devout churchgoer. We were married in church. However, the priest and John got on really well. John had become very involved in modelling, as a distraction, and it was his relaxation away from just being sick. He had a huge shed in the backyard and the priest would come around and would hang around with him for hours. They had their own relationship. Whether it was religious or not I don't know. That relationship developed all the way through his illness. I was dependent on my Sundays. But religion has taken a back seat since then. After John died, I just sat back and thought, hang on a minute. I was too exhausted to make the effort to go and it was a different parish because we moved house three or four weeks before he died. I don't think I have lost my faith completely. I still believe in God and if I hear of someone who is not well I will say a prayer, but I haven't gone back to the depths of my religion. I feel very comfortable with my role in the church.

Towards the end of the first three-month period of chemotherapy he had a bit more, then he was given a break, then he had a long duration, another three months or so of radiotherapy. There was only one session that I didn't go to with him because he wanted to go on his own. He said he wanted to go on his own that one time so I let him. All the other times I would never consider not going because he needed my help to get to the car. During that time there were a couple of people who owed us money, business people, and the minute they found out that he had cancer the cheque was in the mail.

After the chemotherapy and radiotherapy, the cancer had shrunk in size but he never went into total remission. In the first stages of chemotherapy we were told it was shrinking. The slow nod of the head from the doctor would say this is OK but I was still worried. You soon learn the signs and body language. At the end of the chemotherapy we didn't ask because we had to go back and have more tests and more x-rays. They reviewed him then and said he would most likely have to have radiotherapy. From the radiotherapy we had to wait another month or two. In the early stages when he was filled with doom and gloom and depression and the medication was upsetting him, he wasn't very optimistic at all. He was very low. Very flat.

John got very deeply into alternatives at that time and they caused a few problems because I thought he was losing touch with reality. At times they did give him a great sense of strength and made him positive and confident that he was going to beat it. At one stage, when they mentioned doing the radiotherapy, he said, 'No, look at me, I'm doing well. I'm so much stronger and healthier and I'm going to be fine, I'm going to heal myself.' I remember walking down the street from the hospital just arguing with him and asking him not to do that to me and to the children. But he said he was going to heal himself, that he was better. I was a bit desperate then. I said he should not give up.

Before he was diagnosed he was father of the year. He was very close to the boys. Our daughter was at preschool but the boys were at home and the younger one used to love going to work with him. He was always no more than a foot behind him. He idolised his father. They had a very, very strong bond and John had a very strong relationship with his own father, so it was passed down. He was very, very sick when he was sick, but at other times he was really involved with the kids. Most of the time, though, he was really scared—scared of getting too close. He wasn't pushing them away but he was scared of getting too close.

He talked about his fears. He had nightmares. Fears of death and dying. He would tell me about the nightmares but it was mainly the fear of death and dying. In the early stages I was looking up everything on cancer. I just had to know. I had to feel comfortable that I fully understood it so that I could deal with it. He had a dream about death and I was sure I had read somewhere that dreams of death don't symbolise death but to him it didn't matter what I said. His own death was too close and he didn't like it. When you are in that situation, it is really hard to comfort or give security to someone and I think that we just mainly cried. We cried a lot together.

My family and John's family and close friends were fantastic. My mother said she didn't know how I could do it all because the phone hadn't stopped ringing. She knew to pass the work calls on but it was just the sheer number of people who were ringing to wish us well. Close friends became a lot closer. They were wonderful. They'd ring up and if they didn't ring they'd just turn up. Or they'd ring and say they were coming up on Saturday. Or they'd just drop in for tea or coffee. To an extent I always tried to be the stronger one and to be the very optimistic one when he was pessimistic. That was me normally.

It was a terrible time when John's health deteriorated severely. It was around Christmas. At that stage something in him snapped. He knew that he was deteriorating. Symptoms of the illness had come back—night sweats and loss of weight—and I couldn't take any more. We had a terrible time. At that stage we had a lot of debts that had built up because of the business. When he answered the door he'd accept whatever it was, then when he closed the door he would get really angry. Some of the bad luck we had just seemed to get worse and worse. Financially we went through a hell of a bad time because we had a large debt outstanding. We had commitments to the bank because we had just invested in more business. Although most of the employees were very, very good there was no way they could do what John did in the business. We had a sickness benefit policy, but otherwise we were in a terrible way financially.

We were renting our house. We were aiming to buy a house when the other business popped up for sale so we decided to buy that instead. It was getting to the stage where we couldn't afford the rent and we had an argument. I snapped. I'd had eighteen months of it and I just jumped into the car and went down to my mother's place, crying all the way, and got there and said, 'I'm sorry I just can't keep on doing this.' I was so fearful of losing him. I didn't want this happening to me. It was so close to Christmas and it was all terrible. We talked about it and I said he had to get help. He just couldn't keep going in the alternative medicine direction—where he just thought we should pack up and go away and there was no reality and I found it the most frustrating thing—there were the children to think of and finances and everything else. Prior to moving in here, four or five months before, our financial counsellor—who was a godsend—stepped in and applied for a debt moratorium for six months. In that time the business just dissolved.

Once he was diagnosed as terminal, we came home and John said we should get the money from the insurance policy. He just wanted to get away, not to pretend by this stage, but to a warmer climate. He said he was not prepared to just go home and wait for death. I was a bit worried. I didn't know what he meant. We did that and organised to go south for a couple of weeks. He had really started to deteriorate by this stage. He couldn't walk from the house to the shops down the street without needing to rest. At this stage we had accepted death—possibly a month or two before. I think he had accepted death before I had because the symptoms were coming back.

He changed drastically at this stage. In a way I didn't like at all. I remember sitting down and he was talking about it and he was very emotional. He said it had the better of him and he wasn't going to fight it any more and that was it. He became more mellow. His main concern by this late stage was to go on holiday. So we went south to the sun. For the first couple of days we did all the tourist things despite him needing to take rests all the time. We took the children and they really enjoyed it. Before we left, John told me to go out and buy some new clothes. Something really nice. He wanted to go and have dinner at a really smart restaurant. That upset me dreadfully because I knew then that he was admitting defeat. That made me a bit reluctant to go. I was surprised though that he got around so well when we did finally go. We stayed at a lovely resort. He would sit down every now and then and take a break. To see him you may have simply thought he was an asthmatic. It was so important to him to be there in the sunshine. He was so happy.

We had his medical records with us and one day he had to go to the medical centre for a checkup. We had already organised for him to have an oxygen cylinder for when he was short of breath. He used it one day and then that night he couldn't breathe. I heard him turn the oxygen cylinder off and he said simply that he could not breathe. He said he thought we had better go to the hospital. I had asked the doctor back home what I should look for at certain stages and he said to watch out if his breathing became really tight. That's when we should go to a hospital. The same doctor had said it would be good for us to go on the holiday despite the deterioration in his condition. That last stage went a lot quicker than we imagined. We thought he had at least two or three months more. So at 1 o'clock in the morning, there I was, in this holiday resort on the south coast. I rang security and said I was staying in one of the condos and that my husband was a cancer patient and that I needed an ambulance urgently. Then I remembered I had the children with me so the security man brought his wife with him. The ambulance arrived. I followed in the car. We drove for twenty minutes to the hospital. John had tests and they said they would get him breathing and get a specialist in the next day but after being there about an hour, I realised it was 1 o'clock in the morning and I didn't know whether we were there for a few hours, or days, or what. I started to panic.

I rang my sister who was minding our house. She had been my backbone all the way through, minding the children when I needed her and entertaining me. She was absolutely incredible. I rang her, explained that I was thousands of miles away at hospital with John. Well, she was half asleep because she'd only just got back from work but she said she would come straight away. I said I was not simply fifteen minutes away so she said she would catch the first available plane but she was short of money. I rang the airline and told them the whole story. They were great. They said she could be on a plane at 6 o'clock in the morning and that I could pay at the resort. I went back to the resort, picked up the children, drove to the airport, picked my sister up, she dropped me off at the hospital and then she took the kids and did the holiday thing for the whole day. The next afternoon she came down to the hospital and visited us and brought a change of clothes.

They had said he should stay in hospital for a couple of days on the medication and stabilise before we went anywhere else. In the next twenty-four hours he deteriorated badly. His family flew down. We arranged to fly back home to continue the palliative care with a nurse flying with us. We had organised for an ambulance to pick us up from the airport at home and go straight to the hospital. That was when John asked the doctor to leave the room. He said to me, 'I don't want to go to hospital back home.' I said, 'It's up to you. How are you going to handle it? What about the kids?' At this stage we were being organised to fly home the next day. That night he said to me, even though he was now on oxygen and morphine all the time, he said we had not been for our night out. I laughed and he said the best he could do was the hamburger shop downstairs with a couple of cans of soft drink. So we put him in a wheelchair. The hospital was right on the water. We had a lovely time. We sat on the beach with our hamburgers and cans of soft drink and he said simply that it was far better than being in hospital back home.

He went into a coma later that night. He passed away the next day. I don't know if there is any control or mind power in being able to die or not, but there, with the view from his window, I think he knew that he didn't want to go back home to hospital and into that sort of environment. The last stage went on for many, many hours. I was very agitated and uncomfortable about it and I would go outside every hour for about five minutes and cry.

By the time I left the hospital after he died it was early evening and I remember getting in a taxi to go back to the resort to the children—they knew by this stage. The driver, thinking I was a tourist, asked if I was enjoying the place. I suppose I said something like, 'Oh yes, it's a nice place.' Then he asked me if I was visiting someone in hospital in this happy-go-lucky sort of way and I just said, 'Look, shut up, OK! My husband's just died and I'm going back to my three kids so just shut up, OK.' Then I felt really bad because the poor guy had just picked up someone without knowing. After ten minutes I said I was sorry for speaking to him like that and he was crying. I felt so bad. That poor innocent man. I tried to give him a big tip when we arrived, but he didn't want to charge me anything. The next day I felt very isolated because I had to get on a plane and people wanted to greet me and ask about my holiday. It was uncomfortable. Everyone else was just going on with their normal lives. The fact that it happened away from home was very hard, because family and friends were all a long way away.

I came back to phone calls, people. I felt so suffocated. The wellwishers. I had everyone over wanting to do things and telling me what to do. What I had to do was organise the funeral. I had people trying to organise everything, this and that and this and that but I wanted to do it by myself.

The hard part is that when someone close to you is dying you don't sleep for about two months before and then for about six months after. You just keep going on a continual high. I was very busy and very concerned about the children. For a couple of days it was like a vacuum but after a while that disappeared. I thought hang on, I don't have to do a, b or c, he's not here, there's no medication, I didn't have to cook for him, or talk to him all the time, and that was a huge vacuum just sucked out. Also I didn't have a business to run any more. I wouldn't say a weight had been lifted off my shoulders—I know a lot of people say that— but I did feel as though I had lost a lot of the immediate stress and strain.

A day or so after the funeral, I asked my sister what was going to happen next and she said I had three kids, that was what was going to happen. She said I had a brain, that I was bright and I should do a course in computers or something. In that first month or so, when you're in that situation, you just say something and people say do this and you just do it. My way of handling it, eventually, was that I had three children here and I had to handle it to the best of my abilities, for them. I used to wake up thinking I had to actually get up, but how was I going to handle each day? When their father passed away, the children were very upset. They didn't show very many emotions, or burst into tears, but they were young. My daughter at 6 was very quiet and my elder boy was just another little boy. The younger boy was just a toddler. We didn't just cut it all off and pretend he had never existed though. They have an amazing comradeship, my three, and I think it's because of the circumstances they've been through. They are very, very close buddies. Financially, though, things are very, very hard now.

Lately, I have been going out with a girlfriend on Friday nights. She is divorced and hoping to meet 'Mr Right'. I'm in no hurry to meet someone else. As I have said to her, when you have been married to someone and loved them as much as I did and had such a close friendship with them, there is no way you are going to think of it happening again. I wouldn't settle for second best. I wasn't out looking for another father figure. I was going to be independent.

A little while back I needed some time to myself, so I organised for a girlfriend to look after the children and I planned to go to the city for the weekend. Just to go away and have a good old cry and get away from everyone because I needed some time out. So I did exactly that. I planned to have time by myself but I got on the bus and there were only one or two passengers. I had a couple of good books and was prepared for a long ride when a woman got on at the next stop and sat next to me and talked all the way. We had a ball, an absolute ball, for two days. She was divorced. It wasn't what I had planned but we had a great time. It took me a while to talk about being newly widowed but because she was divorced she was happy to talk more about her circumstances.

A couple of months after I lost my husband, I saw an advertisement in a local paper about grief and I rang up to find out about it. I found it hard that there were no other people in my situation that I could talk to. The woman I spoke to said there was an organisation which dealt with the process of grief and that they were trying to cater for the younger age group. I rang them and they said I should come along. I went and I was really annoyed because the next closest person to my age was at least eighteen years older and the rest were in their sixties and seventies and I felt really alienated. But because there were people there who appeared to be worse off than me, I turned my grief around. I began to support them. I still felt alienated because the odds were against me as a younger person, though. There is really no social support other than your own family and friends.

MARY

Mary lives and works on an 800 hectare grazing and cropping property. Now 49, she has continued to run the property and another larger holding further west since her husband Don died of cancer five years ago, despite massive changes in government agricultural policy which she says have caused even further hardship. Mary says it took three or four months after her husband's death for her to stop wearing sunglasses into town for fear of bursting into tears. She also says the day-to-day needs of running a business prevented her from losing her grip and assisted her in the process of overcoming her grief and getting on with her life. As well as managing the farming and grazing business, she has also completed the education of her two sons, one of whom has returned to the farm while the other has moved into the world of high finance in London. On the day we spoke, the sunglasses were again in evidence.

My sons were 21 and 19 when Don died. I was 44. It was pretty rotten. He had cancer. They never found the primary, which I think for everyone was pretty hard to reconcile. Modern medicine hasn't made as many gains as it thinks it has. I think it must be easier to accept if you actually know what you are dying of, rather than just secondaries generally. He died just before Christmas and he had been diagnosed in September. My father died of cancer but he took four years. There's a big difference between that and a few months. The difference is that you know you've got no hope.

I think my immediate reaction, once the cancer was discovered, was to cry. I just cried. He was in hospital. I knew he was going to have problems because he'd had secondaries in the spine for some time and he always had a bad back, but it was obvious this was something quite different. He was very ill. He hadn't been really ill until about a month before the diagnosis. It was very quick. It was one of those cases—like they say, they open you up and shut you up and send you home to die. Well, they didn't open him up, but it was the same sort of thing.

He was 60 when he died. It was extra difficult because the doctors would come and they were all his age. They deal with death all the time and they'd say oh, you're too young, we'll do something. But there was absolutely nothing they could do. They couldn't find out what to treat. Even though they couldn't find it, they knew what sort of cancer it was and they knew where to look. It could have been several— thyroid, pancreas or a couple of others, I can't remember now. They could eliminate prostate because they took a blood count but it was the only one they could eliminate. It's hard to describe how he felt in that three months.

He was on a lot of drugs, including painkillers. He was very bitter with me, which I think from what I've heard—my father was the same with my mother—seems to be a reaction, which I couldn't cope with. I couldn't cope with it at all. He never knew it, but I had to have him put on tranquillisers so I could cope with him. The doctors realised it was a problem. I don't think I could have cared for him otherwise.

He was in hospital in the city for a week and then he came home for about eight weeks. The whole thing went on and on. He had ray treatments for pain relief while he was in hospital. In those eight weeks he was at home, it was a nightmare. It was just a nightmare. You are trying to look after someone who's dying before your eyes. The boys were away studying. They came home on weekends but they were really remote from the day-to-day dying. I coped when I was by myself with Don, I suppose, but when other people came it was pretty trying, especially if they came to stay. The actual physical demands in that situation are quite enormous. I don't know how people do it for a very long time—how they cope.

The other nightmare, of course, was the farm during that time. Don withdrew quite a bit. He wouldn't answer the phone. He wasn't terribly mobile, of course, because by this stage he was on a walking frame. The cancer was in his bones. He withdrew quite a lot but he still wanted input into the running of the farm and we were coming into a tough time. We were having failing crops, but I got some help from a neighbour—and do you know, people are terribly kind. I don't see how people could cope without that kindness and help. The help that people give you in a small community is enormous. People are terribly generous with their time, terribly giving. Whether that's something in a small community, where everybody knows everybody, I don't know. It may happen everywhere.

To be quite frank, you just try to get through the thing day by day. You don't know what's in front of you, so you don't plan. You don't plan at all. I was too busy trying to get through the day and watching out for him. I felt all the time that he could fall—he never did, but he could have, so I couldn't really leave him on his own. The actual day-to-day survival when you're 30 kilometres out of town is quite horrendous. Prior to the diagnosis, he ran the farm on a day-to-day basis and he went about his business in a normal fashion. The three farms were productive. However, we had—and I still have—huge debt. It wasn't that long since we'd bought the last place, the sheep place, so we were quite well in. And that has certainly influenced my activities since he died. It really makes survival that much harder because the first lot of money that comes in has got to go to the bank.

If you are living with someone who is dying, who knows they are dying, who is not particularly old, it is not an easy experience. It's very soul destroying, especially for them of course, because the medication makes them someone completely different. You're not living with the person you knew. The medication totally affects them. They have a huge cocktail of drugs—painkillers, hormonal type drugs, antidepressants—and it changes their personality. Don would be very aggressive with me and that seems to be, from what I've seen, quite common. I didn't react very well to that. I used to cry a lot.

But that was only part of it. The business part made it much harder. It was so complex because he didn't let go. But then, as I said, he withdrew. I know that's impossible to explain but he withdrew and at the same time he wouldn't let go. We had one experience: we were going through a very dry time, our crops were failing and we had a sharefarmer who was bankrupt, which does raise a few business problems, although it was under control. He rang up and named two people he wanted to agist the crop to. Well, they were people who were not going to pay us. And I had to deal with that. And do you know, I actually swore at him. Although now I think about it, I probably would have done that with this chap under normal circumstances. He obviously had no idea about people. They were both conmen. I suppose what I'm saying here is that the circumstances I was in probably didn't change my reaction to things that I had to deal with outside. I think I reacted the same way and made decisions that were reasonable.

Apart from the fact that we didn't get any crops, the actual day-to-day running of the place here was surprisingly smooth. I didn't have the hassles that I could have had. I don't know whether it was pure luck. I wonder about it.

None of those things that could have happened did during the time he was dying. The cattle didn't get boxed and the water stayed alright.

I was 22 when I married. I have no idea where I met Don. Absolutely no idea. He was quite a bit older than me—sixteen years. I'd known him most of my life. He came from a large town and I was from a smaller town further west. He bought a small place out there before we moved here. We came here in 1973 when I was 26. We'd been married for four years. We were able to buy the 2000 acres [800 hectares] here because it was undervalued at the time. It's mainly a grazing property with a small amount of cropping. We farmed it for nineteen years before he died and I have run it for the past five years. We lived in the city for the first few years we were married and I quite liked it, having lived my childhood in a small town. I can't remember much about the early years of my marriage. You probably blot a bit out, don't you? I had children fairly quickly. It was only fourteen months before I had our first son.

Don wanted to come back to the land. He, I think, was more ambitious than I was. He was much keener to make a quid and it was certainly the right move financially as far as the value of the property was concerned. In the next ten years the value of land around here took a huge jump so we made the right decision. Don already had a block just outside the town I grew up in. It was a small block and he swapped that for another block further up in the north-west near the cotton country. I now sharefarm that 3600 acres [1500 hectares]. In 1988 we bought what would have been a soldier settler block about 50 kilometres from town. That's sheep only. Mostly during those nineteen years Don ran the farm. I had the two boys to raise. I did some cattle drafting and other day-to-day things, but I'm basically quite lazy so

I never used to dispute anything much. But as we got more involvement up in the north-west I became more involved down here because he'd be away for stretches at a time. I had to do things down here.

I was basically, I suppose, a negative person, but Don worked on me for the whole time we were married. My first reaction would have always been to say that something might not work—I suppose as a sort of good luck charm that it would work. And my mother is extremely negative. Whether it's genes or environment or both I don't know. But Don worked very hard on making me un-negative. Positive actually. Which I think has probably worked. Although, you know, I think I would have still kept going even if he hadn't changed me. You know why? Because you've got to eat. And you've got to do something with your life. When you're only 44 you've really got to fill your life up with something.

Once he died I suppose I had a few options. I could have sold out. Everyone says, and I quite agree myself, that you should not do anything in a hurry in that situation. I don't think that's an old wives' tale; I think that's quite practical, because no matter what you feel you are absolutely, physically exhausted. It is physically demanding but I was young enough, I suppose, and it didn't last very long with me—probably only a few months. I've never slept particularly well again. That's when my sleeping patterns changed. Certainly by winter I had got over the physical strain. I felt that I had recovered by then. But because of the double whammy—when it's physically demanding to have someone at home and emotionally draining—it is very, very tiring and I do find everybody reacts to a crisis differently and to grieving. The fashion of the moment is that you've got to cry all the time, but that is very wearing. Especially as crying gives me sinus. I used to get it a lot then and I knew I was in trouble and I couldn't cope with all the palliative care people wanting me to cry.

I suppose the options, once Don died, were selling or not selling the farm. But I'm basically lazy. My job was to be on the farm and I was and I still am. I suppose part of the reason I'm still here is that running the farm was always something I felt I would be capable of doing. I had thought about that before Don died. When he was dying he actually decided he wanted to sell here and keep the western blocks for financial reasons. This probably made things quite hard for him, and for us. The boys and I refused—we said we wouldn't do it. I didn't quite know how we were going to handle that. I had refused to move for many years, I must admit. He wanted to go to Hay, Hell and Booligal and I refused. But, when he was dying, I was a bit confused and had agreed to sell the western block so we could consolidate. We were really too busy trying to master what we had. It was quite a conscious decision that we would stay here, quite a definite decision the boys and I made when Don was dying. When he said he wanted me to sell out, I said, 'I can't physically do that at the moment'. That's as far as I got. Emotionally, too, it would have been appalling.

Even before Don was dying, my elder boy always wanted to work in the city in the money market sort of world. Always—since he was old enough to know it existed. My younger son was always keen to stay but how they came to that arrangement startles me slightly to this day. I have no idea if my elder son will ever come back to the land, although I have deliberately kept the options open for him. Some time after Don died, I did make a conscious decision that if neither of the boys came home—one was in the city at university and the other still at agricultural college—then

I would sell the blocks out west but the younger one came home and that's been a tremendous help.

Looking back on it now, after five years, I don't think I coped. I don't think anyone does. I think I probably coped better than most people afterwards because I did accept that Don was dying. I think a lot of people don't. I suppose because I was so much younger, I had always accepted that there was a good chance that he would die before me, but perhaps not quite so soon. I had accepted that. I even went into marriage accepting that. Within a fortnight of Don's death, there was the crutching to do so it was really day-to-day but I am now, only just, starting to think about my long-term future.

It probably wouldn't have taken me five years if we hadn't had the drought. I mean, we've done it tough. I'm sure he would have made totally different decisions to me. I'm sure of that. But the thing is in this five years the rural industry has totally turned on itself. For instance, we hadn't been back in wool long before Don died. The clip is sold at auction and you are sent the valuation. That's a big part of selling wool. I get the valuations and put a lot of thought into reserve prices. Well, when we went back into wool, he'd vaguely come in and say, 'Have the valuations turned up?' and that was it. But you can't do that any more. You've got to be much more detailed these days. Don was much more into the broad-spectrum approach. I don't make decisions I think he would have made. I make my own. I have been known to say, 'Oh, that's what Don would have liked,' but I'm a little bit manipulative. You have to be a realist on the land.

In the past five years I have changed my friendships a lot. Of course you do change your friendships all the time because people change and they have different interests. I have become closer to some of my friends—a few in particular because we are single women, we do things together. I've got some friends in the city—a couple of single women—and they took me to a fête down at the local catholic church and there was a woman there whose husband had dropped dead that week. It was just the same. People were being very caring and supportive.

Support networks have been important to me. Neighbours, friends and business associates have been marvellous. They've been caring and kind and helpful. I suppose my interests haven't changed all that much. I play more tennis than I did when Don was alive. I felt during the last few years of his life that when he was at home I should be there too. We used to socialise together—go to the pictures, go to the city and go to the theatre—he didn't play sport because his back was too bad, although he used to play golf occasionally.

I suppose the one relationship that changed substantially was my relationship with my mother. She worries a lot more. I'm an only child and because I'm on my own so much now she worries enormously about me, as far as I can see.

There's nobody in my life at the moment and I wouldn't ever want to make another commitment for many, many reasons, one being financial. Another is that I've done that—I've been married—and I'm ready for another stage in life. I think I could probably fall in love. Love is different. One could love someone and not be married to them or live with them. I don't think I want to cook three meals a day for someone again. Who does the cooking and washing and ironing? If someone asked me to marry them—I mean, you don't know until you're in the situation—I'm pretty sure I'd say no. I don't want that commitment again. I wouldn't say no to another relationship if he was a pleasant person. I don't know if love would need to enter into it.

I'm pretty extended now just doing what I have to do and I don't think much about those things. The farm takes quite a bit of my life and it doesn't leave me a lot of options at this stage, but I think some time in the future, I'd like to travel overseas. If I were twenty years older it would be different, but I'm not. I've got to make money to survive now. I don't have to worry about twenty years down the track. I don't have a fancy business plan. You throw them out one week after you make them. I do a detailed financial plan once a year, which is something we didn't do before Don died. He whinged and whined for two weeks and he was so proud of his financial expertise and I'm hopeless and now I whinge and whine.

Interestingly, my relationship with institutions such as the bank didn't change, which surprised me. I spoke with my accountant and he said he didn't think I would have any problems—it was mothers passing farms down to sons where there were the problems, apparently. With wives taking over it doesn't seem to be much of a problem. I wonder if it's because we're so conservative? I have wondered about that.

When my father died, my mother lived in the city and she didn't have the same experience as me. About three months after Don had died, I'd at least started to go to town without my sunglasses on because people had stopped making me cry in the street. Then I ran into this woman and she cried on the post office steps and we weren't close or anything. She just stood there and cried. And all I could think was, God, I didn't bring my sunglasses and here we are crying again. It was interesting because while we had friends in common, I'd never been to her house and she'd never been to mine. That, I think, shows the depth of feeling in a small community.

What I couldn't cope with was people actually physically in the house. We had a huge number of visitors—people popping in and staying in the house was hard work. I was dependent on my neighbours for shopping and other things. It was interesting watching the people who came and the people Don responded to. It was quite surprising. Some people I thought he would like to see he didn't want to see. Others he felt comfortable with, but they weren't always the ones I could pick. He was on twelve-hourly medication with morphine so I had to wake him, then he'd go back to sleep and I'd go out on the ag bike and check everything. Then I'd come back in and give him breakfast and then he'd shower. After an hour or two, I'd get him lunch and he'd have a nap, then he'd stay up quite late watching television, which we fought over. That's when my sleeping patterns changed. I did a lot of yelling then. But I suppose I always did that. He'd just get the huff.

Our marriage was relatively happy, I think. Basically happy. Not everything was a success. It wasn't a brilliant marriage but I think it was average quality. I probably changed a bit during the marriage—in fact, probably a lot. I think I got more definite. I think I coped with Don's actual death as much as anyone could. I didn't have a lot of feelings at the time because I was exhausted. I was actually, physically, exhausted. And mentally exhausted, but particularly physically. I was keyed up waiting for a long time before he died. He only spent a few days in hospital before he actually died.

I don't think Don would have wanted euthanasia. We never discussed it. I couldn't have done it, I know that. I couldn't have actually told someone to administer a life-killing drug, although I wasn't actually at his bedside when he died.

Despite all the physical exhaustion, I did think I would come through it. With the grieving and the loss, I suppose the longer it is the less you feel. You tend not to think about it so much after a while. Your life's moved on, and I think that in itself is very sad. You never think about the actual time it took if you can avoid it. There are things that I come across that he did, which may be work related, and I might want to change them, so I think about him then and I tend to think about the happier times, not the dying time. About the only thing I've changed in the house since he died was to burn some old cheque butts. I've put new covers on the lounge but I should have put new covers on the lounge a long time ago.

On the farm I've made enormous changes—management changes that government bodies and the American government have enforced on us. The house is the same but the business is certainly not and I do often wonder how Don would have coped with this nitpicking finely tuned sort of management. His management style was to keep it simple and it's much harder to do that now. He would have been 65 now, but I don't think he would have devolved any responsibilities to our son, who has much more responsibility than his mates who still work with their fathers.

Wellwishers are an interesting breed to deal with. It's probably hard for people to understand, but once you've seen a wellwisher you've seen them. It's over and it doesn't matter any more. There's an initial thing of seeing people, but once you've done them once it's much easier. Everyone actually becomes a wellwisher but once you've seen them it's OK. You have all these physical hurdles. Wearing sunglasses helps. It's interesting, because once you've gone through it yourself, you don't know whether you should be a wellwisher or not. You don't know whether you should talk to someone or not because you know what they're going through. You've got to see them, but it could be a matter of years.

It's taken a long time but I've accepted that Don took a lot of his despair out on me. I suppose I really accepted it at the time, but I found it hard to deal with. I wasn't dying and he was. But I found it very hard when he did take it out on me. I'm fairly pragmatic and I think that probably helped. I've noticed that the older and younger widows I know are by far the most pragmatic. The middle-aged ones seem less able to cope because their lives were their husbands'. They don't seem to have much purpose for themselves without their husbands. I still felt I had a purpose. There was a reason for me to exist after my husband died. I keep thinking I'm in the second half of my life and I think Christ, that's appalling. When you think, well, I've done 50 years and I'm not going to do another 50, it is pretty startling, I can tell you. But it's not as difficult as dealing with the death of a husband. Your own death is something you pretend is not going to happen.

After Don died, I did miss the companionship. There's no one to tell things to. I notice I do tell things to my son now and what's even worse is he does it to me. It might be gossip, or something funny, but I don't think that's terribly good. This relates to the change in our relationship. Before, he was a student. Now we work together. A lot of the time he is telling me what to do and calling the physical shots around the farm. The stability of the farm is helping me keep going, I suppose. I wonder, if my son started to make major changes, whether I would try to block them because it would be taking away my stability?

I consider myself a widow. It makes me laugh. I think it's a funny word. I mean you don't run around talking about widowers. I think I'm referred to as the widow in the community. I don't know if it's a very nice label. Being a widow is a different world though. I have friends now whom I wouldn't necessarily have had were Don still alive— women who are older, whom I've gravitated towards, probably because they are in the same position. It's a bond of circumstances, widowhood.

MICHELE

After twelve years of marriage, Michele and Denis decided it was time to start a family. However, tragically, around the time Michele conceived, her husband was diagnosed with cancer. For a short period after the birth of their daughter, Denis went into remission, only to succumb to the disease ten months later. Here Michele talks of the three and a half year battle she and her husband fought and a few years later the shock of discovering her daughter suffered from attention deficit disorder. She also tells of the change in her life, nine years on, when she met and married Gary, despite her belief that she would never enter another relationship.

When my husband Denis died, we had been married for thirteen years. Before that we had been going out for five years. I was 36 when he died in 1988; he was 35. We had deliberately put off having a family because he was at university studying law and I had a career. A couple of years prior to making the decision to have a family, he had decided to become a barrister. Now, unless 'daddy' is a QC, doors don't automatically open for you so it's pretty much a matter of going back to the bottom rung. Denis had made that decision and we were struggling, like most young people.

Later in our lives, after the twelve-year mark, we decided we would start a family. I was 33 when I fell pregnant, but I had a miscarriage. Six months later I fell pregnant again. With the first one, at the eight week mark, I had haemorrhaged a lot. The same thing happened with the second one. I was ready for another miscarriage but for some reason it didn't happen.

When I was about four months pregnant, however, Denis was diagnosed with cancer. Now, I mean that didn't just happen suddenly. He hadn't let me know: I was unaware, mainly because of my involvement with being pregnant. I hadn't realised he had not been feeling all that terribly well. He had in fact discovered a lump in his groin which I knew nothing about. I had gone interstate on business—I worked for a metropolitan newspaper—and while I was away Denis was off seeing the doctor. At that stage his practice was just starting to come on nicely. He was getting a bit of cash flow going. When I got home he announced that he had this lump in his groin and he had to have a biopsy.

When you are pregnant, the feeling of expectation is there and you think nothing could possibly happen. But the unthinkable did happen. He was told he had non-Hodgkin's lymphoma. It had only been a few days since he had the biopsy. He rang me at work. My husband was very matter of fact. He said the tumour was malignant and he had to have chemotherapy. It totally knocked my socks off. Words cannot describe the shock. He had been working at home. I got in the car and I have absolutely no recollection of the actual drive from the city. I was just a total and utter jelly. I remember I came into the house and I couldn't find him. It was a wet, miserable day. It turned out that we had a leak and he was up in the ceiling fixing it. I was in a daze. I was totally zonked. It was probably the worst shock of my life. He was very matter of fact about it and he was like that until he died. I was a mess—a total basketcase.

The next day we had to go to the hospital and be told the realities of what was happening, which was six months of chemotherapy. He was very stoic. He had a tremendous regard for the medical profession. He tended to do exactly what he was told. Suddenly people came out of the wood-work and started telling us about alternatives to chemotherapy, but when we put them past him, the doctor said, 'If you don't have the chemotherapy, you'll be dead in six months.' Denis said that was it then, he'd do it. He didn't really countenance any of those other things. He had a healthy regard for the medical profession and was prepared to do what had to be done.

Fortunately I was physically very well, in terms of my pregnancy, from then on, but it was totally fraught with worry. I was devastated. In hindsight I don't know whether my child suffered, but I have since found out that a lot of the goodness I was hanging on to she might not have been getting, although she is a healthy child. I had to put on a facade of strength from my husband's point of view. We had to make quick decisions, such as whether he would go to a sperm bank and donate sperm for future babies. We were fortunate enough to have one baby and I think we were so keen to get on with the job of the treatment that we didn't pursue the sperm bank idea in the end. We thought we were fortunate to have hung on to one, which was an all-consuming thing.

After he went into remission I thought it would be nice to have another child and I was almost naively thinking we would defy the medical gurus and accidentally fall pregnant. Every month I would think, maybe I would just fluke it. But of course that didn't happen. And with hindsight it is better that it didn't because ten months later he was diagnosed again. He didn't handle the chemotherapy very well because his blood had a problem. He was in hospital a few times. He had been healthy but he had sinus and an eye problem which was fairly rare and because of that he had been on a long course of steroids. One general practitioner suggested the steroids may well have knocked his immune system down but I will never know. He was a solid man, 180 centimetres tall and, apart from the eye and sinus problems, fit and healthy.

While he was on chemotherapy, he tried really hard to go to work but there were days where he was unable to and as he progressively lost his hair he looked sicker and sicker. A lot of his work and his solicitors dropped away and I guess he could understand that because he was fighting a battle with himself. We discussed it and I think privately he felt perhaps there had been a loss of confidence—not in him personally, but in the situation. However, there were matters he kept going with. There were other friends who were happy to keep briefing him despite it all. I would have to say the momentum of his practice was affected. I was working and the organisation I was with was very supportive of my situation. I was healthy enough to continue up until about two weeks before I had the baby. That was a good thing because it did take my mind off the stress. I would drive him into the city then drive back and park at my work. There were lots of afternoons that I had to leave early, on the days Denis was having treatment. When his blood levels got terribly low, they had to put him into hospital. But work was a good thing. I would advocate work for surviving. It helps enormously if you throw yourself into it.

Denis finished his treatment a couple of week before I was due to have the baby. He was terribly ill. In fact, he was hospitalised and the doctor said later his blood was at such a dangerously low level they were going to lose him that week. I hadn't known that. At the same time, my own father was dying and I was doing the shuttle between hospitals. My doctor was getting angry with me because my blood pressure was going through the roof. My father was 78 and he died the day after my daughter was born.

Earlier, Denis and I had enrolled in pre-natal classes together but he was far too sick to go so I had to go alone. It was just awful because it was another reminder that this was not an ordinary pregnancy. There were the other couples together doing exercises on the floor and there I was on my own. Even now I feel sad that we were both cheated of a happy period of expectancy. It was just such an anxious time.

Anyway, the time came and I started to contract. It was 11 o'clock at night and Denis was out of hospital but feeling dreadful. He took me to the hospital and he was so ill that I told him to go home because there wasn't really anything that was going to be happening for a long time. I sort of laboured on, on my own. It would have been good for me to have him there, but it wouldn't have been good for him personally. So he went home and came back the next day and he was there for the delivery.

My father dying the next day was very traumatic and I couldn't go to his funeral because I was having feeding problems and was still in hospital. Denis went to it. The baby was wonderful. She brought a lot of joy to our lives, which were otherwise fraught with tremendous worry. At the time I was feeling pretty positive generally, I suppose, because Denis had finished his chemotherapy. The overall prognosis of the doctors was that the chemotherapy had knocked the cancer out and at the very beginning he was given an 80 per cent chance; they said if he was going to have cancer that was the best one to have. So while he had survived, he had to get back on his feet and over the next six months he did get better and a lot stronger.

We were hoping that it would all be behind us. Denis was going along every month to get checked. We were in a major rehabilitation situation. He was also trying to recapture the practice. There was still an element of uncertainty and it was like having to start again, but he was happy to do that.

Life then was generally a rebuilding process. I had made the decision to leave work after sixteen years and not take maternity leave. Neither of us wanted me to do that because I felt I just wanted to be with my daughter for at least the first three years. We put my payout into the mortgage and Denis was able to make ends meet on half a practice.

About ten months later he was diagnosed a second time and that was almost worse than the first diagnosis because when we both went in to see the doctor he said Denis was not going to survive. He said he might have at most two years. They had discovered a lump under his arm. Unlike the strength he showed earlier, this really knocked him about. In fact, it really knocked us both about. This was not something we had talked about during his remission: we hoped it would never eventuate. We had spent our time trying to be positive and Denis had been feeling better generally, although he never really was the same. The chemotherapy took its toll. That was the worst fear. While we were hearing that he had two years, there is something in you that makes you think that it is not going to happen, that once again you are going to defy the medico.

Denis was more concerned that he was going to have to go through chemotherapy again and lose his hair. He found that a totally demoralising experience: he had actually suffered quite a bit of comment. He could be walking along the street on the way to the station and young boys would sing out from a car, 'Hello baldy'. It was extraordinary. You would not expect, as a mature person, to have to encounter namecalling. It was amazing. You lose your eyebrows and you do look like an unwell person, whereas there is a difference if someone has just shaved their head. Losing his hair was the one thing he did not want to come to terms with at all and we were almost relieved when the doctor said they would not put him on intensive chemotherapy. They decided to put him on a monthly low dose. He was told he would be able to work and probably lead a normal life. That's what effectively did happen for the first twelve months. He was on a low oral dose and he was able to work. Then he started to get very tired. I think he gave up the idea of trying to save his dwindling practice. He felt it was too much of a struggle, especially with the long-term prognosis.

It was about that time a close friend offered him an associate partnership in a firm of solicitors. He made a decision to sell the Bar practice and try to pay off the house which, with hindsight, was a very sensible thing. He went into the solicitors' firm, where they were happy for him to work on a weekly wage. He didn't have the stress or worry about running his own business. He was able to work for another six months. They were very good to him, but after he died I didn't see that much of them. His friend had a family and other things to get on with.

He made the decision to leave because he was getting progressively worse. This was a 35-year-old man who had had the world before him. He was still very strong mentally and very stoic about the prospect of death. I think he went through a period of bitterness. He especially didn't want to know anything about religion. He went through a lot of depression. Friends wanted to sit down and talk about alternatives, but he wasn't really interested. We did have a young minister friend who would call in. He was a very academic man and Denis liked him. They used to toss the issues over. Denis was brought up as a Catholic, but he was never what you would call practising. I was brought up a Seventh Day Adventist and we have very definite views about death and the life hereafter, but I didn't try to talk to him about any of that because I don't think he wanted to discuss it. That was fine. I could understand that. If I had been in the same situation I think part of me would have been pretty bitter as well. You feel you have been given a major knock in the teeth.

I used to cry about it because I could see what was happening. He would come home and he was always bringing presents. He also insisted we put in a new kitchen. I didn't want to know about a kitchen—it was the last thing on my mind, but he wanted me to have a kitchen. He was wonderful to me and our daughter who, by this stage, was nearly 3. Fortunately from about 2 onwards someone had suggested hiring a video camera, so I did. I took lots of footage of him and her together, three hours at her second birthday party. Whether he twigged to what I was doing I don't know. I had taken a lot of still photographs of them together but I took it to record her young life as well because a lot of relatives were here so it was an appropriate occasion. I made sure I took a lot of him and I am very glad I did.

As you see your husband declining before your eyes, you have to think of things like funerals. He had been brought up a Catholic and I was Adventist but his family and mine have always been very close. He had to make a decision and I had to find out what his wishes were. We had never discussed this aspect. I didn't know what to do but you have to face these realistic problems when someone is dying. We had made out our wills and all our other affairs were in order, but we had never considered funeral arrangements. We were too young. And I didn't know if he wanted to be buried in his church or what he wanted. I agonised over this for months. It was only when I spoke to our minister friend—who has since died of a brain tumour—that he said I should simply ask Denis. He was very matter of fact. He said he wanted me to cremate him. It turned out he liked this minister friend so much he was happy for him to do the service and he was happy if I wanted to do it at the church where I took my daughter. He didn't have a problem with that but I didn't know how he was going to tell his parents. I felt they were going to be very upset. It was his decision, so I asked him to tell them because I felt very uncomfortable about it. He said it was fine: he would talk about it the next time they were in.

He didn't die any creed, but there was a point in the last few months where he dropped a lot of the bitterness. He was feeling more amenable to there being a God and I don't feel it was a last-minute bargaining situation. I think when you are dying and when you are with someone who is dying, up until a certain point you are resisting the fact that it will ever happen. It is a denial situation. But there was a point for both of us where there was a total acceptance. When you do finally accept that, a certain burden is lifted from you. You are still exploring alternative methods, going to clinics out in the country—and we did a few of those things earlier on. I had him on diets, I read all the books on alternative healing, and he was happy to go along with it but of course he never would have gone against what his doctor suggested although we did a bit of everything towards the end. We ate so many carrots it wasn't funny. We had carrot juice coming out of our ears!

I think you come to a point where you just accept that it is going to happen and there is a certain relief that you don't have to fight it any more. He somehow became close to God by doing a lot of reading. He didn't go into it with blind faith. He read the Bible and saw something there that he felt comfortable with. He died with the peace that there is perhaps something ahead. He was able to read a lot about that and feel comfortable with it. And that made me feel a lot more comfortable.

He actually died in hospital. A couple of months before, he had been kept on painkillers. With dying people they manage pain with certain drugs. Once you go on to the morphine, it is usually a rapid decline. It is an arduous business, watching someone die. I never thought I would have to go through it. We agonised through a whole night at the bedside—the vigil—but a few days before that, he had lapsed into unconsciousness. Before that he used to ring me up every morning at 6 o'clock. One morning I found it difficult to communicate and I knew then I had lost him. After that he was in and out of consciousness. You wish then they would just give it away. What's interesting is that it's a physical struggle to hang on to life and yet when you are watching someone go through it you want them to give up the fight.

At this stage our daughter was 3 and, apart from knowing that daddy was terribly sick, she was a young 3. I didn't realise at that stage she had a problem. The only hint we had was that she was very active and that we could not read a story to her because she had no concentration. Other than the fact that daddy was terribly ill and would not be coming home from hospital, we didn't talk much about it. She was not communicating very well herself. She didn't verbalise a lot of what she was feeling. It might have been better had she been a little bit older, or even been a baby, because she was at a very difficult time. I am sure she was affected, but she couldn't tell me how so there was a bit of a behavioural problem for the next six months.

After Denis died, I put a bit of a survival strategy in place. I kept the mail in his name so the postman would not twig to the fact I was a woman living alone. You do feel vulnerable. I used to try to leave little clues out that there was a man living in the house but it backfired once because somehow, after he died, I had omitted to advise one of his credit card providers and it was renewed and stolen from the letterbox. I got a bill for $3000, which was very unpleasant. Tradesmen would come to the house and I would say I had to talk to my husband. That went on for a long while. I never owned up to complete strangers that I was living here alone with a child.

I think it is very important to be able to talk about the whole thing. I know members of his family were not able to and I think it was hard for them. They were not able to get everything off their chests. I had been crying for three and a half years. I had, in the privacy of my own company, bawled my eyes out. I had been on my knees, I had pleaded with God, I had sobbed—especially when Denis was out of the house, because I couldn't really do it when he was around. I remember when I was pregnant and I hadn't finished work and I used to go into my boss's office when he was off in another city on business. I would take the filing, lock the door and cry my eyes out. I didn't want to do it in front of others at work. My boss had a Bible in his side cabinet and I used to pick it up and read some of the Psalms because they are some of the most comforting words you could read. I would sob and sob then I would get myself together and go back out to my office and try to act normally.

I think by the time my husband died I had cried so many tears and it had been such a long struggle, that there was a sense of relief. Even getting used to the fact you don't have to go to the hospital any more is a relief. Cancer is such an all-consuming thing that there is almost a sense of relief that you can look ahead. I had a 3-year-old daughter and life suddenly took on a normality—like going to the supermarket. There were feelings like those despite the fact that the funeral was such a terribly sad occasion. I was very cried out by that stage. I spent the twelve months after he died in total shellshock.

In the first couple of months, I had so many people write to me I spent at least a month writing back. People were also very generous. I had people send me very large cheques, mainly established people who said they felt there was nothing else they could do for me. It was very overwhelming. The Bar Association arranged the funeral and offered immediate help with my daughter. Some of my former bosses also sent me very large sums of money from themselves and their wives, which was overwhelming. The firm Denis worked for at the end gave me part of their annual bonus. He had been gone a few months at that stage.

Denis had an insurance policy, but I didn't know what financial situation I was in for some time. A week before he died, Denis said from hospital that he had left some money in his jacket pocket in the wardrobe. He was thinking about me even then. I had been running the house and there were no real problems financially. I knew I would probably have to go out to work. The upshot was the house was paid off and there were a few investments but not enough to give me income to live on. I was secure but I had no money. I really wanted to stay in the house. I could have sold it and moved into something smaller, but we had liked the house and put a lot of effort into it prior to him getting sick. It was also my one major security. If I had sold it and bought something cheaper I could have invested the money, but I would not have had enough. I felt a need to hang on to it from a security point of view. I decided to see what happened for the first few years. All I knew was that I would have to start looking for a job of some sort.

My daughter had just turned 3 so I started to work part-time at a school. I had been a secretary at a corporate level and there was no way in the world I could do that—work the long hours that were expected. But I was offered a part-time job. Fortunately the local preschool was prepared to take my daughter five days a week so I would drop her off and go to work from 9 o'clock until 2.30 then pick her up. It worked reasonably well for a few years. The income kept the wolf from the door, but I thought my requirements were going to become greater and I felt that I needed to retrain. I didn't feel I had the luxury of time to be doing something part-time at university. I had to do something radical.

Interestingly, at the time Denis died and when I was getting financial advice on how to plan the future, I was very surprised at the number of people who actually said look, you are only 36. There is a good chance that perhaps you will get married again. These were mainly professional people. They were telling me that one of my options was to get married again and that I should consider that seriously in order to survive my widow situation. My first thought was that there was no way in the world I would ever contemplate meeting anybody who could possibly fill my husband's shoes as a person. Part of me felt like saying, 'Sure, look I'll just go up to the pub at the end of the street, there's bound to be somebody there who can, you know, who I can grab.' I mean, I was there seeking financial guidance on how to handle the situation I was in and I didn't really consider that remarriage was a solution. It certainly wasn't something I was actively pursuing.

I suppose I hadn't really thought of myself as a widow. I thought more of myself as a sole parent, perhaps because about this time various people started to twig to the fact that my daughter was a very active child and there were some milestones that she wasn't meeting. I tended to not place a lot of emphasis on them. She was healthy and that was far more important to me. She was conceived while my husband was in the early stages of cancer and I was always more worried about that.

I enrolled her in a school nearby to where I was working. In her first year the school was not entirely happy about some of her developmental aspects so I had her assessed and it was found that she had a lot of learning difficulties. I found this very hard to deal with. But what I didn't realise was that this was the beginning of a long line of things for her—she was incredibly active and even at eight we had behavioural problems. At about age 9 she was diagnosed with attention deficit disorder.

These children are hyperactive, totally inattentive, often very non-compliant with authority, and impulsive. I was certainly going through these things with her at home and I realised later that the school was going through these things also. We've tried medication therapy and it has modified her behaviour to the extent that she is on a much more even keel. Prior to this she had no quality of life. All her teachers, her relatives and her friends have noticed a real difference. She is now acting like a normal little girl, although she still has a lot of learning difficulties.

In amongst all this I still needed to address the ongoing financial situation. I never wanted to be on a widow's pension. I didn't want to be a statistic of the social security system. I wanted to be as independent as possible. I had been, I suppose, a career woman up until I fell pregnant and I was rather surprised that I chose not to take maternity leave. I didn't want to have my child minded. I wanted my husband to get back on his feet. If he had stayed well I would not have gone back to work. After Denis died I knew that it was going to be a long haul. I had help with minding my daughter from my elderly mother and sister but that was not a long-term proposition.

A friend talked me into contemplating a career teaching at technical college. The teaching aspect appealed to me and I was going to be teaching what I had done in industry. I did external courses for a couple of years, four nights a week studying, to get myself in the teaching door. The money was very good and I felt that it was a sensible thing for me to teach because I was still working three days a week. I had dropped the five-day job and took a three-day job so that I could teach at night. I have been doing that for a few years now.

The good thing is that the system is flexible enough for me to still have time with my daughter. I could have elected to take a high-powered personal assistant job but then I would have had to use day care. I still wanted to be a mother. I have still been able to have enough time with my daughter either end of the day. The two part-time jobs have given me the flexibility to be a parent, which I really always wanted to be.

I would recommend that anybody in this situation should try and hold on to their independence. It provides a feeling of satisfaction and it gave me something to aim for, something to focus on, a new career and a feeling of achievement. While I had a good part of myself focused on my daughter it wasn't a healthy thing to be 100 per cent focused on her. I needed something else. I still wasn't the slightest bit interested in a relationship, seven years after Denis died. I didn't have the time nor did I have the energy. Some women who were married used to say I was so lucky because I was independent. They said I could do my own thing. I think they thought I had a life even though I didn't have time for a relationship. I had girlfriends I went out with. I have some wonderful friends, although it's interesting because some of them did drop off. Some I haven't seen since Denis died. But they have been mainly couples. On the other hand there are two chaps next door who were just neighbours but they have been absolutely wonderful. They have developed into best friends. They are almost like my guardian angels.

My advice would be that if anybody offers you anything, swallow your pride and take it. It doesn't mean you are giving up your independence. People really want to help. You do have to draw the line, though. I had someone who said he was going to come and mow my lawn every week and I said no. He had his own home and own family. I was determined I was going to be independent of things like that. I was going to pay to have things fixed. But in saying that, there were people who went behind my back to do significant things and I guess I swallowed my pride and accepted those offers of generosity. That was wonderful. One friend got me a magazine subscription and she has been renewing that every year. She thought it would be a nice thing for Michele to receive in the post and sit down and flip through on a lonely night. Little things like that are really nice.

I have now remarried. Gary is someone I technically went to school with although I wasn't looking at him back then because he was a couple of years younger. He was divorced and had been supporting two children. He asked me out in the middle of 1994 which was right in the middle of my big career focus. He knew that I was a widow. He rang me and asked if I would like to have dinner. There had been a few occasions where I had been invited out. They were people that I had known and I used to think well, there is no good reason why I should not go out to dinner. So I did. It was nice to think that, at 43, I was still being asked out. That was lovely. I always felt particularly uncomfortable though because I felt I was on the wrong side of the table with the wrong man. While it was pleasant I didn't want to necessarily go out with them again.

I pretty much felt like that with Gary at first, too. I thought he was a really nice fellow but I didn't see much long term in it. I was not feeling that I wanted to launch into any sort of a relationship. I thought he was a nice guy and that was it. In the end I said it was not that I didn't like him but I really had to get on with my career. I really didn't have any inclination—I didn't have any energy and I didn't have time, frankly. So he drifted off for a year or so. At the time I was probably getting all the satisfaction I needed from the new teaching career. It was early 1996. I felt comfortable that I was doing an adequate job. Also I had to make a decision about my daughter's medication. She hadn't gone on to it at that stage and it was an extremely difficult decision to make. That was a big thing for me to deal with.

Two years later Gary and I met again. I was a bit less stressed, a bit more relaxed and had a bit more time available. He started to ask me out again, even though he was a good 40-minute drive away. Once again, on going out with him I thought he was a really nice fellow and I couldn't think of a good reason that I shouldn't. But I did clutch my handbag for four months. I wasn't ready for a physical thing. I never ever thought it would come to that anyway. Whenever I was with him I clutched my handbag. I didn't want him to get anywhere into a situation where he could grab my hand. I was totally defensive. I think he was probably aware of what I was doing and he was a thorough gentleman.

Maybe at this point I was starting to loosen up and think it was nice to have some male company. One night we were having dinner. I told him right from the beginning about my daughter's condition. He actually asked, while I was proceeding to talk about what a full and active life I had and how in control I was in, if I had contemplated letting someone else in to help me. I was taken by that. I thought, no I haven't. I fobbed him off. It was not an option, I thought. He was so totally different to my husband, which was interesting. He was not academic. He has an automotive background. I liked the ballet, he was into car racing. You couldn't get two different people. But I thought he was a very nice fellow and I had a great deal of respect for the way he thought.

I think maybe—and I can admit it to myself now—after nine years I was probably getting a little bit tired of being superwoman. Even though I may not have admitted it then. It was lovely having someone to open car doors for me and equally nice for it to be happening at 44. He was a very thoughtful person. He didn't overwhelm me with it but just occasionally he would be out in his vehicle during the day and he would call into the office with a bunch of flowers. It was lovely getting something like that in front of everyone. It was starting to get a bit embarrassing almost, because it was four or five months and I was still so definite in what I wasn't going to do. I was starting to think that I would have to call it a day. I was actually the one who eventually made the first move. I asked if he was going to hold my hand and that was very daring. I hadn't kissed anybody in nine years. It turned out that he was probably just as nervous. He had been divorced about the same length of time I had been a widow. He had been out with a few other woman and had serious relationships, whereas I hadn't even kissed anyone. Even though I had been out to dinner, I had found very clever ways of avoiding being kissed at the front door. I got that down to a fine art. I didn't ever want to be in that uncomfortable situation.

There had been times when I had thought about the loss of the physical relationship but I was so dog tired most of the time. From the time my husband was diagnosed to the time he died our sexual life had totally dropped away. That's the time you find out just how strong your relationship is. I missed it of course. We also went through the stage where he was in remission and he was trying to regain those aspects and it was extremely difficult. There was a certain amount of readjusting and he was never the same. It knocked his whole body around. There was a psychological aspect to that as well. Women have got to be totally understanding. I think I was. Fortunately I was consumed with a small baby and I was pretty tired. But it is one of the important side issues.

With Gary I would say it started off with a friendship and there was never any pressure on his part. Denis and I had only ever had one short conversation about the future with regard to my welfare. He said to me one morning in bed that he had been thinking and that it was fine with him if I remarried. He added that I should make sure whoever I married would be a damned good father to our daughter. He was thinking about the child and who was taking his place. It had been playing on his mind. Gary didn't overwhelm us because he didn't come on too strong. He was wary of her up and down days. He had been through a trauma with his own son, who had lost an eye at a very young age. Little things were important. I had to send my daughter on a camp and I had never done that. I was worried about whether she would get her medication and Gary was able to come up with practical solutions. He said, for example, that he would go on the camp as a counsellor just to make sure she got her medicine. I thought that was a wonderful gesture. Would you put your hand up just to go on a kids' camp for a week? There were lots of little situations like that.

At the moment I am facing a situation where I am thinking of withdrawing her from school for six months to put her into an intensive literacy program to try to give her a really good kick start. I have been wondering how I am going to handle the transport arrangements to get her across the other side of the city and get back to work in the time. This is the sort of guy Gary is. He said he would take six months' long service leave, which he had owing, so he could take her to and from the school every day. He is a terribly thoughtful person who cares about me and cares about the package deal. I didn't delude him in any way, shape or form that this little girl was going to be easy to bring up. In fact I tried to talk him out of it because our relationship did develop further. It was something I had not expected. He has been able to take on the package and it has made many of those issues a lot more bearable.

I stopped clutching my handbag eight or nine months before we were married and the relationship blossomed. I got to like him more and more. He still brings me flowers. We went to Hawaii in August which was the culmination of a nice year because my elderly mother had put aside a lot of money for my sister and me a long time ago. She wanted to see us go overseas together. There was enough for me to take my daughter. My sister and I did in fact go together and it was coming up to that trip that I thought I didn't want to go because I was leaving this wonderful man and I felt like a bit of a teenager. We sort of decided a week before I went. He was supposed to be going on a holiday to the United States with a friend so we decided instead that we wanted to get married. It was a quick decision. All the problems I had put forward as issues just didn't seem important. Not in the slightest. He didn't mind the prospect of taking on this child with ADD so we arranged to get married on our last stop, which was Hawaii. My sister brought my daughter home that night and we stayed an extra week on our honeymoon. We are still trying to amalgamate his furniture into the house. He has moved in here because it seemed the most appropriate thing and it is also less of an upheaval for my daughter. We talked about the fact that he would be moving into the house I had shared with Denis. I didn't have a problem but I think he had to think about it for a while. We have now overcome any problems and he has even watched the video of Denis with my daughter.

I have always been, and continue to be, close to Denis's family and they have accepted my decision and welcomed Gary as part of their family. It has been rather a nice ending because I am now on friendly terms with Gary's first wife. She brings his children here when they come to stay so she comes in and has a cup of coffee.

I still have happy memories of my first husband and this house. I probably came to terms with all that very early because I wanted to stay here. There were some relatives who had difficulty with that—some of Denis's relatives found it hard to come into the house. I have never had any time to be bitter. That would have rubbed off on my daughter. I had a house to keep going and life had to go on. I won' t say there were not times I didn't get sad. Something would remind me of things we had done together. Even now when I make decisions about my daughter I try to think what Denis would have done. I think I've been lucky with men though. I think I've won the lottery twice. Gary is not trying to take Denis's place but he is a very good friend to my daughter. I have very strong religious beliefs and faith but I don't play it entirely by the book. Gary is the same religion. I will never understand why Denis died at such a young age. I was brought up to believe in the life hereafter and I will continue to believe that, but there is no guarantee that life's crises aren't going to affect you. I don't think you are immune to them. I think they can bring you enormous comfort and in my case God has provided a soft landing, in some respects. He has given me the stamina to deal with it and to advance my career. I could have been in a much worse situation. I suppose you never really know what's around the corner.

There are two ways to die. You either have a long struggle and then the person dies and I think you are probably a little more equipped to deal with that because you have been conditioned. Then there is the other one where it is a complete and utter shock and then you are left with a tremendous void. There was no shock factor in my situation to deal with. We were conditioned to what was going to happen. It was a three-year struggle.

My mother, despite the fact she is 87, continues to provide me with the inspiration to keep going. She is one of the best friends I have ever had. They say that these things don't happen to people who can't cope, but that's ridiculous. We don't have our hands up saying these things should be sent to us because we can cope. I don't think anyone would put their hand up for that. It doesn't do anyone any good being full of remorse and wallowing in self-pity.

NANCY

Since her husband's death, Nancy has remained living in the house she shared with him for almost 50 years and in which they raised three sons. Her husband Alan died of a heart attack the day after returning from a two-week stay in hospital. Nancy talked to me about the things she believes equip a woman in older age to live the remainder of her life after the death of a partner and why one would consider remaining in the matrimonial home. She also spoke of the emptiness, the void in the physical relationship and the need for closeness even in old age, along with the special problems she believes women encounter after the end of a long relationship.

I've been saying it's eight years since Al died, but I think it's nine. Isn't that awful? How easy it is to forget these things as you get older. He had a heart attack. He'd had emphysema and asthma all his life and he had a heart attack and went into hospital. He was there a fortnight and he rang up on a Friday and said, 'I'm coming home.' It worried me because I knew he was still getting angina pains. I thought he wasn't well enough, but you don't argue with the hospital.

So he came home Friday and a neighbour who lived next door came in the next morning and sat with him. It was Saturday and he was out there in the sun in his dressing gown. They were chatting away, then later on I said I wanted to go up to the shops. So I left Al sitting inside watching the football on television. He seemed comfortable enough. I went up to the shops, but they didn't have what I wanted. I started down the escalator and I got a most awful feeling. It was horrible. I thought for a minute I was going to faint, and I hung on to the banisters and went down. I went home as quickly as I could. I was only out about half an hour. I opened the back door and said, 'I wasn't long, was I?' There wasn't a sound. You get the most awful feeling. There's just still air. I went into the bedroom. Al was just lying back on the bed in his pyjamas and dressing gown and he had just gone. He had some bits of pill, white pill, on his tongue, just on his lip. He had evidently had a pain, taken his pills and gone to lie down and that was it.

Of course, I was horrified. You bring them home from hospital and they are supposed to be getting better. This was the day after. He came home on the Friday and this was on Saturday morning. So I rang the doctor, who was just around the corner. He was covered in paint. He said he had been painting his house. Anyway, he came around and he was shocked too because he had seen him on Friday night. He had come around to fix his medications then and he didn't believe me when I rang up. I said he looked quite peaceful, I hoped he hadn't had a lot a pain. 'Oh yes, he would have, it would have been a big heart attack,' said the doctor. It was what he called a myocardial infarction. So it would have been painful. But Al was just quiet. It didn't look as though there had been any struggle or anything. He was just 72 and had suffered from asthma but not heart problems. His father died, I think, when he was about 62. He went very suddenly. I don't think he had heart problems before but Al's elder brother also went suddenly with a heart attack.

They took Al to hospital by ambulance when he had the first heart attack and I drove over afterwards. He was here at home when it hit him. I've more or less forgotten what happened. He got this pain. The doctor came around—I think it might have been late afternoon—and ordered the ambulance, then off Al went. He spent two weeks in the hospital. I would go over every day. At the time I thought he mightn't come out of hospital. I don't know a great deal about hearts but he was still getting angina pains, even there, while he was in hospital. He said, 'They're walking me up and down the stairs' and he didn't seem very happy about it, but this is what they do now with heart problems. They get them on their feet as soon as possible. Anyway, he was improving a bit then all of a sudden he rang up and said he was coming home. He was booked in on the Monday to go back to the hospital for a stress test but he died on the Saturday.

When I found him, I said, 'Oh, Al' and kissed him on the forehead. I rang the doctor, then I rang my eldest son. He was on the golf course but my daughter-in-law said she'd ring through to him. I then rang my other sons, I think. I can't remember too clearly now. Anyway my eldest came over and we arranged the funeral together. That was it. My daughter-in-law was splendid. She arranged the food for people to come back to after the funeral and she said any time I felt like I wanted to come over for a meal that I was welcome. They weren't living far away at that time. I used to babysit for them and Al used to go over occasionally. But there wasn't much empathy between us. I think I've probably only kissed her about ten times in all those years. She's not a person who will come in and put her arms around you.

I think Al loved me more than I loved him. He was very, very affectionate. I think I basked in that a bit. He couldn't walk past me without patting me or stroking me or cuddling me. We would walk along hand in hand sometimes, like you see some old bods. I always held his arm if we were walking along. He'd always put his arm around me or give me a cuddle. That's one of the things I miss most, the affection. I miss the sexual relationship too. Even though I'm in my eighties now, I still miss it. But you've just got to get over it. I think Al loved me right till the day he died, really. Marriage I suppose becomes a comfortable relationship later on. I think that happens later and that's why people continue living with each other. Al had a bad temper but mine is fairly hard to get going—I've only lost my temper a couple of times I can remember. Al would flare up. He used to slam the door. I would think there was no good me losing my temper. You wouldn't be together very long. I'm fairly patient and tolerant and Al was a bit intolerant. But we worked together pretty well. I think we had a very happy life except when my middle son got polio when he was very young. That was a big upset.

I was four months older than Al. We were married in 1942. Fifty-six years. We were married the day Darwin was bombed, but we didn't know. We left the reception and someone took us up to the train—we were going to the mountains, of course, the place of honeymooners—and we didn't know about it until the next morning. I met Al when he was in the same group of young people I used to swim with when we were about 17 or 18 down at the beach. One day he asked me if I wanted to go to the pictures. It started from there. We left the seaside because Al was advised to. His asthma wasn't good. Before we were married he used to get it very badly. When we moved up here I think working in the open—he put up fowl-yards, dug gardens and we planted all the grass—improved his well-being out of sight. Our first son was two and a half when we moved here; he was born in 1945. The other two were born here.

Religion wasn't much help when Al died. I felt I had to face up to it and be strong enough. Al had a very strong faith. I've never been a deeply religious person, although early on my family used to go to church regularly. When the kids arrived they went to Sunday school and later when they were confirmed either he or I would go every Sunday with them. I think I fell out of religion, if you could say that, when my middle boy got polio, when he was seven months old. I used to go up and pray madly at church and I'd come out not feeling as though I'd ever been there. I didn't get a lift like some people do. I think you have to have a terrific lot of faith, and I really didn't. You wonder about the beginning of the world, and science and God just don't seem to mix somehow, do they? I am Anglican but my eldest boy changed over to Presbyterian because his wife was when they were engaged. Al was terribly hurt about it because this went on before we knew about it. I think Al was more distressed than I was. I don't think religion helped me. It had never played a big part in life and I don't think I did very much praying or anything like that when Al died.

We did a lot of things together during our married life. We did most things together because neither of us belonged to clubs. Before we were married we went to the younger-set outings on weekends and things like that and we played tennis together. Tennis fell away after marriage, because the boys were all away at war.

Al was in the militia. He went to war and his asthma got worse. His doctor at the time said he shouldn't have been there. Al was just under six foot [183 centimetres] tall and fairly solid when he was older. He was always fairly slight when he was younger. He had retired at 64 because his chest was getting bad again, and he found travelling in the train difficult, in the summer. He started in the bank when he was 18. He had done his real estate exams and he got into the valuing department. That meant he was out a fair bit and he enjoyed that, but then his health went down and they put him back in the office and that was where he retired from. He just couldn't cope with it any more.

I worked for a year after he retired. I was ten years at the council and then I left. When our youngest was about three or four I used to go in and do a day in the copying office occasionally. When he was bigger I got five years at one of the big public schools. Then Mum died and she left her house on the coast between the two of us, me and my brother. He gave me a cheque for half the value. I'd never seen so much money in my life. After I got the money I said I didn't need to work every week so I enrolled with an employment agency. At this stage all three children were at school. Most of the work was in the western suburbs so I started going over there and I'd work two weeks and then I'd have a couple of weeks off, which was good. One of the jobs they gave me was at a large electronics firm. I was asked to go on the permanent staff and ended up being there for eighteen months. I was very happy there. I was there five years because you had to retire at 60 then.

We went away in my holidays, up the mountains and down to the southern highlands and Al would play golf and I'd take the buggy around. I played golf too, earlier in the piece, but not after we were married. He found that the buggy on the hills was a bit heavy so I'd pull it around. What I wanted to do was get a caravan and travel when he retired but he wouldn't. He said no, we only had a four-cylinder car and it would be too much strain for it. By this stage our eldest son was married, the middle one was living in the eastern suburbs and the youngest was still at home.

Al got interested in hydroponics at this stage and we had three hydroponic gardens. I've got photos of the most enormous cauliflowers and beans and things. He was very happy there in the garden. I bought a deep freeze and he grew all these marvellous vegetables and we froze them. The gardening kept him so happy and it didn't take too much energy. We didn't belong to any clubs or other organisations during the ten years he was retired. We were quite happy going out for a day in the car or working in the garden. He'd be working up the back and I'd be weeding down the front.

We went on a long trip the year before he died. We wanted to find out if we would be happy doing that sort of thing and he enjoyed it, but the long days—out by 8 o'clock and not back until 6—were tiring. They do rush older people on tours. When we suggested a shorter day they said that people wanted as much as they can get. But we enjoyed that trip. The next year we thought about travelling overseas, but we went on the train out west. It was a railway excursion that went from Monday to Friday. Some of it was a bit much for Al. It was hot and dusty. Al didn't like the heat much. His chest was getting bad and he was developing diverticulitis, a bowel complaint which causes a lot of pain. During that week, he had to lie down a fair bit of every day.

We hadn't travelled much when we were younger. We couldn't afford it. Sometimes we couldn't even afford to go to the coast and see Mum—two lots of buses and the trouble of toting three kids, and at Christmas when we had presents to give them Mum and my brother hired a car to come up and pick us up, and then they took us back home again.

Al was always very short of money. They didn't pay very well in the bank. That's mainly why I started trying to make a little bit. I did embroidery at home for a while. A neighbour across the road was doing very fine embroidery for an old friend of hers and she introduced me. I used to sit at home and do that for very little an hour. It annoyed Al, I think. Then another neighbour, she started making little plastic pilchers. She introduced me to that. I'd be sitting here and they were like a string, like the festoons on a ship, all joined together and I'd cut them off in the end and they'd be all over the place, pink and blue and white. This was what Alan walked into at night after he came home from work. It did bring in that little bit extra though and that helped.

After we moved in here I never thought about moving again. We were quite happy here. I did hope we would travel more but, as I said, Al didn't care for the caravan idea.

Now that I'm older I've got my name down at a couple of retirement villages but that's only because I knew a couple of people who went to those places and I rather like the area. This was always home, even after Al died. I never thought of moving out. My main worry was keeping the garden the way he liked it. I didn't do a lot of planting. I just concentrated on keeping it tidy. There was a lot of work. I dispensed with three gardens. That was less to mow around.

I have not made any great friendships while I have been living here. After my middle son got polio I was on the bus three days a week going down to the hospital for his treatment. The other days I'd give him exercise and trot up and do the marketing with him in the pram. Going to the pictures was the only real break I had. When the boys were bigger and in the scouts we got involved with that and we used to go square dancing. We had a marvellous time. There was a scout ball and everything. Al was secretary of the scouts for a year and then I went up and took shorthand for them.

After Al died, I had to make a conscious decision to get more involved in things. I woke up one morning, about five months after he'd died, and thought well, Nance, this is it. This is what you've got to deal with. You've got to snap out of it. You're by yourself. You've got to do things. Al always did the household expenses. He'd give me money for the board and he'd do the electricity, the rates and all the rest. I didn't know anything about that. But after he died all these things kept coming in. I thought well, I'd always managed my own money when I was working. I bought a little secondhand car and paid that off myself and then bought a second one and I'd always managed the repairs. What was left over from my wage went into the housekeeping and clothes. After Al died I began to think of myself as an independent person and that everything that got done was what I had to do. My two youngest boys were living else-where and the eldest was married. It doesn't matter how close you think you are, they've got their own lives and they don't often consider that you may need them.

Just after he died, a neighbour asked me up quite a lot and at Christmas she asked me up for a meal. She has always been very good to me. My next-door neighbour was also very good. She'd ask me in to meals but I hadn't made very many friends. I'm 82 now and a lot of my neighbours are much younger, with young families. Not that I have a lot of neighbours I know, they change so much these days. Al had some great mates from work who he used to go down the coast with regularly. After he died I didn't see too many of them. We were both very fond of a fellow Al had worked with in one of the branches and we had known him for many years and were friends with him and his first wife and then his second wife and I still have a Christmas lunch with her every year. She'll send a card and write, 'What about our lunch?'

Sometimes it's not until February or March, but we do have it every year. She doesn't drive so I go up and see her. We've always been very close and we talk about our families. She's in her early eighties too.

I've been lucky healthwise. I garden more than I ever did and I do the lawns so I suppose that keeps me fit. It's not stressful: I don't do it all in one go. I don't over-exert myself and I do it early in the morning or late afternoon so I'm not out in the heat.

Al died in June but we had always meant to go off to the mountains to the gardens in spring. I used to belong to the retired association of the place I worked at and they were always sending out notes about visits. We went a couple of times with them to the wineries and to the snowfields—just overnight as a rule. They were a good crowd but nobody from where I was at the time I retired, so I only knew one person. Anyway, a note came saying they were going to the gardens in the mountains in November and I thought I would go. The note arrived about six weeks after Al died— about the same time that I had decided that I needed to get on with life. I went down to get on the coach and the first person I saw was the woman who used to work with me—the only one I knew. She'd only retired that year so we sat together all the way and talked and went around the gardens together and on the way home she said she belonged to the local Probus club. She said they were a nice group of people and she invited me to go along and said, if I liked it, I was welcome to put in an application to join. So I went along, I think it was in the next ten days or so. I went along and I enjoyed it. You know, a very nice crowd of ladies and we had a speaker and they were going to have an outing on a riverboat within a few months so I put my name down for that and I put an application in and it's been all go since. It's been marvellous.

Then a friend whom I worked with was deciding she didn't like being in her home unit by herself. She was getting a bit nervy so she decided to go into a retirement village. It was a church village. A lot of people who were at church with her also joined Probus. They also went into the retirement village so that was how I first decided to go and have a look at it for myself. One day I will have to move from here, I suppose. I liked the look of it. She only had a one-bedroom unit which would drive me up the wall—not enough room when you are used to a house. I thought I'd like a two-bedroom and of course they were like gold so I went and saw the secretary, who said they didn't have any two-bedroom units. He said I would have to wait about ten years for one. He said he would put me down for a one-bedroom and possibly a two-bedroom if one came up. I said I would be ready to move in around three to five years, but I think that's already about four years ago. I could go into a unit here somewhere. They do have nursing staff on hand and a hostel I can go into if I get tired of cooking for myself. But they don't have a hospital, so if I was ill there I have to go off to another hospital, and I would be way out of my area there. My friend is still there and a few more have gone to the village from Probus.

They had a few five-day outings and my friend invited me on those. I'd drive over to the village and park my car there and go away for five days with them and it was wonderful, they were a bright crowd. It was a small coach that took about 30 and we had a lovely time. The fellow who owned the hotel where we stayed came up with the bus to the retirement village and collected us. We went up the coast for five days and he'd take us around all the sights. I really have the best of both worlds, not having to live in a retirement village, living in my own house still, but having the contact and all these outings. I think it will be different once I move there.

I suppose the path I've taken over the past nine years is really very different to the direction we took in the ten years of retirement that I had with Al. We had no particular outside friends. We were insulated but we were happy doing what we were doing. In a weak moment I had said I supposed when he retired Al would probably want to go to the mountains to live. He always felt better up there. His chest got better. So when he retired he went up there and contacted real estate agents. I got a bit scared because it meant going to a completely different environment where there were no friends. We bought a corner block right down towards a lookout. We paid rates on it which were as high as in the city, and we had to clear the block every two years because of the bushfires. Al thought we would sell it, he said eventually he thought I was never going to go up there. He knew I didn't want to go because by then the grandchildren had arrived and we would never see them if we lived too far away. But he loved the mountains so much, I felt awful after. Al didn't push the issue but I knew he was disappointed. So we sold it. I think we only had it a few years.

After a short while being alone ceased worrying me. I don't get tired of my own company because I can go to the pictures or I can pick up a book. I read a lot of books, five or six a week I suppose. I don't read the newspapers. I just listen to the news on radio or look at the telly. I occupy my time pretty well, I think. I have a lot of sewing and alterations to do. I buy things that don't quite fit because I'm an odd shape. They all laugh at me at Probus because I say I bought a new dress and they'll always ask what I'm going to do to it. It's always something. I don't like the shoulder pads or it's too wide on the shoulder. I used to always make my own and I made for other people when I was first married. I used to do a few frocks for people I knew, so that if a thing's not right it hits me in the eye. I live pretty much the same as I did before Al died. Probus has kept me on an even keel. I got two cats six months after Al died.

I suppose I've never really thought about another relationship since Al died. Sometimes I suppose I think oh, I'd like to meet a nice man and go away for a trip but I don't know. I suppose it just depends on what you fill in your days with. I mean there are ladies in our club who are living in a second relationship. They're not generally as old but there's one who's 80 next year and she's got a grand-daughter and a daughter and she's living with a gentleman who's got a daughter and grandchildren and they travel round the country a lot. I don't think it makes any difference how old you are. There is always that need for companionship, for physical contact and for love. If you have a happy relationship, I suppose you look for more of the same. I think if you had an unhappy relationship, perhaps with a fellow who knocks you around, you might not want to go near men for a while. I would be happy just to go off travelling. One of my friends lived quite near us before we moved here and she used to go abroad all the time and have a marvellous time—she loved men after she was widowed.

I've had a very healthy life. I was always the healthy one in my family. I've got the outside interests I've already mentioned and my health, so I don't see any reason why I should move from here. When we bought this block it was nice and big and had trees all over it and it seemed like a good place to have a family. I would like to stay here as long as I possibly can.

When he was in hospital, Al was quite hopeful. He was feeling better, you see. We didn't talk about the fact he could die. It never entered his head. I thought he might not come out but I don't think he did. I'm sure he didn't. We never mentioned it. I'd ask how he was getting on and he'd say 'I went right up a flight of stairs today'. He was quite cheerful about it and longing to get home. Every time he was in hospital with asthma or something he was always keen to come out. I suppose everybody is, really. The only thing he told me to do that last time was to keep the hydroponic garden going. He was happy to get home. He was chortling away with a neighbour up the back in the sun on that Saturday morning.

I remember Al lost a pruning knife that he used and I found it years after he died. I dug it up in the garden. I picked it up and I stood up ready to go inside and say, 'Al, look what I found.' You know, for a moment, he was back again. You never sort of lose them in a way. I still talk to him. I find myself saying, 'Oh Al, look at that', even nine years later. He's sort of there and he's in the garden. That's not the reason I stay here, though. I think the time will come when I'll look at it and think I can't carry it on any more. I'll find I can't do this or I can't do that. I don't do a lot of heavy stuff in the garden. Digging is fairly easy. I'd be happy to go somewhere else as long as I had a little bit of green. I wouldn't like to go into one of these new places that are just flat and you look across from your window and there's just an alley with a window on the other side. I'd hate that. I've been here nearly 50 years. I like the trees.

RITA

After 27 years of marriage, Rita's husband Frank died of a heart attack in Canada in 1972. Five years later, in 1977, after being urged by a friend to go on a tour of the Rocky Mountains, she met and eventually married Bill, a recently bereaved widower from Australia. Rita and Bill have now been married happily for 20 years and, as Rita says, while there was great love for her first husband, she feels she was extremely lucky to meet a man she considered herself able to call her second husband. Rita spoke to me of the grief associated with the knowledge that her husband was dying. She also spoke of the joy that occurs when a widow finds herself in the lucky position of marrying a second time to a kind, loving man.

Deep down Frank knew things were worse for him than he was making out for some time before he died. He would never let me know, though. He had given up smoking for a short time while he was in hospital. He had been a very heavy smoker but when he was in hospital, friends would go to see him and take him packs of cigarettes, and there they would be, sitting in the drawer beside him. When I would go in he would have a cigarette and, of course, he shouldn't have. When he came home he still smoked. He was not a big man. He was very slight up until just before he had his heart attack. Then he started to put on weight. He'd gone to the doctor in February and he'd been told then to watch his blood pressure and his weight. He wasn't really what you'd call overweight but the cigarette smoking didn't help. His own doctor wanted him to stop. That was February, and in July he had his heart attack. I always remember him telling me to advise anyone, if they keep getting headaches and getting tired all the time and worried, that those were the signs.

I was 49 when he died. Two years before, my mother had died at 84. In July 1972 my father died. He was 87. Then in November, Frank died. It was a terrible year. When Frank had the heart attack, when I saw him in the hospital and he was able to really talk to me, he described it as like having a lot of worms in his chest, crawling about with the pain. For about a year before he died he would get the pains so very badly. I would telephone the doctor and he would say to take Frank over to the hospital, which was close to us, and he would stay in the intensive care unit, for maybe one night, until it all settled. Sometimes he would be in longer. There was one time when he was in for about a week just to get himself stable. It started about a year before he died and then right near the end it seemed as though they knew he was not going to come out of hospital. I still tried to be optimistic even to the very last.

He went in on a Wednesday, if I remember correctly. He was still there on Saturday, which was Halloween night, and during the afternoon my daughter came with me to see him. I had asked her if she wanted to come back that evening to see her dad, and she had said no, because she thought he was going to die. I disagreed, saying he was going to be alright but she wouldn't go back with me. While I was sitting with him in his hospital room—he was in a room by himself—I was doing a cryptic crossword and I had come to a word where the answer was dread, and I had just said, 'Oh, I've got it, Frank.' I looked up at him and noticed he was holding his chest. I asked him if he was OK and he just shook his head. I dashed out and got the nurse and the next thing I knew everyone was rushing into his room with machines. They sent me out. I was holding his hand a moment before but they wouldn't let me stay. I don't know how long it was. It seemed like hours. They finally came out. I was just standing in the hall. The nurse said to me, 'I'm

afraid we couldn't save him.' I said, 'Do you mean he's dead?'
I didn't know what she meant. I had wanted to be with
him. I felt very angry that they had sent me out but I didn't
say anything. I asked if I could go in and see him. And there
again, I wished I had said something to the nurse. She held
my arm. I wanted to go in by myself and I was trying to
take my arm away but she was still holding on to me. We
went to the side of the bed and I just touched his arm and
all I said to him was, 'Oh Frank.' I don't think I said anything
more. I just wished they had left me alone with him. I
telephoned some friends to tell them because I felt that I
couldn't drive home but when I think about it now I feel
I probably could have because it was only a ten-minute
drive. The friends came over and drove me home. My daughter had a girlfriend in the house and as we walked in—she
was in the hall—she just looked at me. She dashed upstairs
to her bedroom and her friend went home. I tried to get
hold of my son because it was the day of my grand daughter's birthday party. But they were out at a friend's place
and I didn't know the telephone number. As it happened,
the chap whose house they went to was the son of another
friend, so they came over right away to stay with me. It was
about 11 o'clock by the time we got hold of my son. He
stayed the night with us.

When I started going to work again, I was amused when I
would see on TV, or read in books or the newspaper, about
how some man had taken over the job of a woman—had
become the 'househusband'. Frank was doing that back in
1961. I would come home and the meal would be ready, the
washing would be done and he would have hung it out. The
neighbours used to get such a kick out of seeing him
hanging out the washing. The only thing I didn't let him do
was the ironing. I didn't trust him to get it done right.
Gradually as he got stronger he would make himself go for

a walk—just the one block that we had to go, up a slight hill to get a loaf of bread, just so he would get out and walk. We managed for twelve years after his first heart attack and gradually, near the end, he was getting the pains in his chest. He was then on medication for angina and he had to take regular doses of nitroglycerine which was placed under his tongue. I think by then he thought that he was going to die more than I did. I tried not to think about it.

Our daughter was growing up, but our son had already got married in 1969. During that year, his first daughter was born. My daughter was still only 13 in 1972 when Frank died. My grand-daughter was 3. Frank's relationship with his grand-daughter was not that strong because they were only able to get down to see us on weekends. Both of them were working. We would see them as often as we could but by that time Frank was getting a little bit weaker. He had these periods during which he would suffer Meniere's Disease, when he would have terrible vertigo. In fact, one night I found him on the floor and the doctor came over and gave him a needle for motion sickness, an injection of gravel.

Even after the first heart attack—he had smaller ones later on—he still carried on with the soccer league. He went to Montreal to a meeting once. I went with him on the train and just before it left he had an attack. He took a tablet and went to lie down in the sleeper car. When we arrived he had gotten over it. His interest in the league was very important to him. At the time I never thought about what would happen to me. I know I would come home some nights wondering what I would find. My daughter would come home from school earlier, so she would already be there. She had to go through all of this from the time she was a baby. Frank was even changing nappies when I first went to work, as she was only 2. They were very close. When she was 11 and knew about puberty, he said one day she came home from school and she said, 'Today I'm a woman.' She could talk to her dad. When she came home from school the two of them would sit down at the kitchen table and have a cup of tea and a biscuit. It was good for Frank too: he looked forward to her coming home. He always helped her with her homework but there were times when, being a great one for maths, he would do it one way and she would say, 'No, Dad, we don't do the work like that any more.' But he was very patient. He didn't have a temper.

I was 23 and Frank was thirteen years older so he was 36 when we were married. We had a very, very happy marriage. We had two children, a son and then ten and a half years later we had a daughter. We had a stillborn girl in between. Frank had his first coronary in 1960 when he was 52. He was born in 1908. Our daughter was born in 1959 so it was the year after her birth and for a year he was in and out of hospital regularly. When they did finally let him come home, he was told to only work part-time. The firm in Toronto we both worked for, where we had met, where Frank was employed as a paymaster, went bankrupt while he was in the hospital. He knew it was coming and I think this could have brought it on. This was in 1960. In 1961 we decided we had to do something financially. He was involved in soccer and was secretary-treasurer of the National Soccer League and he got an honorarium, which helped us a bit. We lived in the house that my parents had sold us so we didn't have to worry about payment of the mortgage on time. Owning your own home was the thing in Canada in those days. My father had been a builder and he had built the house. It was he who told me, 'Always own the key to the door and you won't have to worry.' My son, unfortunately, was never interested in playing soccer. Frank used to play soccer in England, when he was a boy. He was from London. My parents came from England also.

Frank and I met at work in Toronto. I worked as secretary to the owner of the company and Frank was the paymaster. During the Second World War, he had more than 1000 employees to prepare the pay for. He was really sharp. I would help him on Saturday mornings in the pay office and we got to know each other. He was 36 when we married and he had never been married before. He was medically unfit so he couldn't go to the war. The reason was that when he emigrated to Canada it was during the very bad depression in England—I think he was only 18 when he went across. He made his way out to British Colombia and they were forming the Mackenzie Papino battalion, as it was called. He joined up and he went to the Spanish Civil War and fought against Franco in 1936. He was against fascism and communism. There were a lot of writers fighting against Franco, such as George Orwell and Ernest Hemingway.

Frank was badly wounded at the River Ebru, I think it was. In fact there is a book that my son found in the library which mentions his dad's name. Frank said he saw so much suffering in Spain. They had no uniforms for the troops. Sometimes there were no shoes on their feet.

When he came back to Canada he still had a brother and sister in England but during the London blitz he lost track of his sister and his father. His mother had died when he was quite young and his father lived with his sister over there. His brother joined up. He was in the navy during the war. The father, sister and her children lived in an area which was heavily bombed and he lost track. The Red Cross couldn't find them, so he never did hear from his sister Lillian again. For a long time after his return, Frank didn't want anyone to know about his being there as people always thought he must have been a communist. Even where he worked he kept it quiet as it was a war industry business. He was the last one who would ever have been a traitor to his country. Of course, Russia did help the side he was on, so right away he was called a communist.

He was a very kind man. A kind and very considerate man. When we met, he was still undergoing treatment for this horrible big hole in his left arm where he had been hit with a dumdum bullet. They used those in the Spanish Civil War. When he first came back to Toronto he was undergoing all kinds of operations to get all the shrapnel out of his arm. Even after we were married, pieces would still be coming out of his arm. It was painful, but he never said a word. We met because he couldn't join up for the Second World War. He enlisted, but because of his past wounds, he was rejected. We knew each other from about 1941 and the war was over in 1945. That was when we got married. I had been engaged before to a chap who joined up but I found out that he wasn't being faithful so that ended. Canada was very much like Australia, a relatively small population, but we still sent a contingent to the war. We didn't suffer as Australia did. We weren't bombed. We used to drive by a little hydrostation and see soldiers looking excruciatingly bored marching around, wishing to be off fighting, but they just had to guard.

We were married for three and a half years before our son was born. I thought he was never going to come. He was born in 1948 and I stopped work after that. Then we had the little girl, stillborn, and then ten and a half years later in 1959, my daughter was born. Frank was getting very involved with the National Soccer League. It was while he was watching a game that he suffered a very bad heart attack. Luckily they got him to hospital. I wasn't there as I was home with my daughter. She was only one year old. I was 38 then.

After that first heart attack he was in hospital for five weeks and when he was released they said he had to take it easy. In those days they didn't have pacemakers or bypasses; they just said to take it easy. Other wives, whose husbands had had heart attacks and died after being home a while, have told me since that they couldn't cotton on to the idea that they should think of their children. Frank wanted to see as much of his children as possible.

We waited a year to see how he would be and I got myself a job through office overload, where they send you out to different jobs. At first I only worked in the mornings then, when he seemed to be managing all right, I got a job near where we lived, in an office, because I kept up my secretarial skills. With Frank being secretary treasurer of the soccer he would have to take the minutes and he would come home and dictate them to me and I'd take them down in shorthand and then type them up. We had a Gestetner there, an old thing, and I'd run off copies for the members. So I kept up my skills even though I hadn't worked in a job between 1948 and 1961. I had only worked from when I graduated from high school with my senior matriculation and went to business college—secretarial college to give it its fancy name—so it was 1940 when I started work. I'd only worked eight years before my marriage.

Frank's wish, which he had put in writing, was to donate his body to science. At the time I accepted that he wanted to do it but when the local newspaper had asked him earlier if he wanted his family notified of when the memorial service was to be held, he had written 'No' in big letters because he didn't want us going through the whole thing again. I suppose that was fine then but since, after I'd calmed down, I thought I would have liked to have had something to remember him by. He was well known in the soccer circles and people would contact me and want to know when the service was. It was written in the paper that donations should be made to the Heart Foundation instead of flowers. He died on Saturday night. I didn't go back into work and Mary didn't go to school for a few days afterwards. We thought by Wednesday we could do it.

It was November, the start of winter, so we still had Christmas to go through. It was difficult, but my daughter-in-law's parents were very good. Because our grand-daughter was just 3 we didn't like to make it a sad event. My daughter-in-law was the eldest of six so they had this big family and they invited us to their place for Christmas. We went over for Christmas dinner and stayed while my daughter joined in with some of them who were her age. My son married quite young—he was 20—so his wife's brothers and sisters were all that much younger. Somehow we got through that Christmas.

Some time after Frank died my daughter noticed in the paper that there was going to be a memorial service for all the people who had given their bodies to science during a certain period, and 1972 came into that time. So she got in touch with them and found out where her father's ashes were. I never had done this. When you donate your body to science they use it as a cadaver for the new doctors to learn on. I was assured that there would be no violation, no way that they would not take this in a scientific way. Frank said to me when he first filled out the form, 'You know, I won't know anything about this when it happens.'

I continued to work, which was another good thing, as I didn't have time to grieve. When I was at work I would have to dash suddenly into the ladies room, close the door and have a real good cry. Then I'd get over that and go back into my office. At this stage I worked at a university. I had a very good boss. He would ask me if I was sure I wouldn't like time off. I only worked Mondays and Tuesdays, but then I started going into work on Wednesdays as well. Then one day, all of a sudden, it hit me and I thought I could not go into work at all. My daughter seemed alright going to school. She had a very good teacher who she could talk to. My brother and his wife usually went down to Florida for a month every year. So I phoned them up and asked if there was any chance of getting a little unit right near them for a few weeks. For some reason you can get very angry at the person who has died. I would find myself thinking, 'Why did you go and leave me? I've still got my daughter to bring up.'

Frank had always been very careful about money. He made me do all the banking and handle cheques and savings and he used to buy government bonds, so I had that to help me. Just before he died, he had asked if I would like to go away for a weekend, up north. When we say up north I guess it was about a two-hour drive. That's just the time when all the leaves are in colour. It's beautiful then. So I made a reservation at a lodge and I thought it was wonderful. We would have holidays in summer but never go for a weekend anywhere. It just seemed as though he knew that maybe this was the last time the two of us would have time alone together.

The possibility that he was going to die soon would come up in the way that he would say to me, 'If anything happens to me, you are young, you get married again,' and I used to say, as most widows do, that there was nobody who could take his place. That's how I felt. I think too that if you have had a happy marriage, you may want to be married again.

It's nice to feel you have somebody that cares for you. I think, being much older than me, Frank understood me very well. I think in my case it made the marriage better.

Frank was not a religious man. He called himself an agnostic. I went to the Anglican Church and was christened and confirmed. My religion changed in one way after I had married Frank. I joined the Unitarian Church. They don't believe in the Trinity, they believe that Jesus was a human, a man, a good man and we should follow his teachings but that he wasn't the son of God. I accepted that when my son was born and I had him dedicated—he wasn't christened. He went to Sunday school for a while but he objected so much. He said his Dad was at home and he wanted to be home with him, so I gave it up after a while. Frank was an agnostic but he never objected to me following any religion. I think it followed from his involvement in the Spanish Civil War. That was why Frank was happy to donate his body to science. There was no other belief in a supreme being.

He didn't have a real family upbringing. He was about 7 when his mother died and his brother was two years older and his sister younger. His father and his sister went to live with an aunt in London and he and his brother went to live with a grandmother outside London and they just didn't have that closeness. It wasn't until after we were married that I said I was going to start writing to his sister-in-law. He never bothered writing but he gave me the address and we have never looked back. That part of the family has always kept in touch.

The only thing that I regret is that neither his son nor his daughter saw his body after he died. He was at the hospital when I came home and I got a call from the university about it and they asked if I would mail the papers. They said they would do all the rest. It was a university teaching hospital. I never saw him again. The men who fought in the Spanish Civil War who were part of Frank's battalion had a plaque and a memorial service for all those who had died. My daughter went and met some of the men who had been there, and I think it helped her.

As far as friends were concerned, there was one couple Frank had boarded with when he came back from Spain who were very supportive. They lived just outside Toronto about an hour and a half's drive east. I would go out there and visit. A lot of friends were older, or to do with the soccer, and after a while I didn't see them that much. I had a girlfriend who had been widowed much younger than me. She was widowed for ten years and she was then starting to go out with a chap. She remarried ten years after her husband had died. It was sad because her husband had been through the war as a pilot. He had not been wounded but came back and then got cancer. He was only just in his forties and had left her with two young daughters. Her remarriage to a boy she had known at high school unfortunately didn't work out. In my social group I still had the people I worked with and I used to go out once a month with my next door neighbour, even before Frank died. We had a little group of women who did sewing and knitting and I still had that to keep me occupied. I still had my daughter, who was occupying all my thoughts. She had teenage years to go through. Of course, drug problems were only starting then. I remember hearing about drugs from a friend and being thankful I had not had that to go through.

About three years after Frank died, a girlfriend who had remarried would invite me around and there would be friends of her husband's there for me to meet. She wanted me to marry again but I said I was not interested, I was still grieving for Frank. That was two years before I met Bill. I was not as angry with Frank by then. I would just think, 'Frank, why aren't you here to help me with this?'

We still had the house we had bought from my parents. About a year after he died, my daughter and I realised there was a lot to do. We had to shovel snow and there was the garden, the lawn to cut and everything that needed repairs. My son was living in an apartment and it wasn't too good for my grand-daughter, who was 3. It was way up high and if she wanted to go out and play they would have to take her down to the little playground. So I discussed with my son the idea of me going into an apartment and he said 'Well Mum, if you want to do that, we'll rent the house from you and pay you whatever your rent is going to be.' This worked out fine. We stayed in the same area so my daughter could go to the same high school. We could walk right to her high school so we decided that that's where we wanted to stay. My son bought the house from me and the mortgage payments paid the rent. Every year the rent went up, so he would unfortunately have to pay more.

While all this was going on my girlfriend was still trying to get me to find somebody. She was one of the secretaries at the girls' college where I worked—I had left the university by now—and one day she asked if I would like to go and see the Canadian Rockies. Neither of us, even though we lived in Canada, had seen the Rockies, because they are way over on the west coast. She managed to convince me, so in August 1977 we both signed up for an eight-day tour. Meantime, the wife of the man I was eventually to marry had died in April the same year. Before she died she had planned a similar tour and though he did not want to go alone, after his wife died, Bill's family—so I found out later—talked him into it as they thought it would be good for him. As if that was not fateful enough, he then got a call from the travel agent to say the trip that he and his wife had planned had been cancelled and another put in its place. Again he started to back out, but encouraged by his family he eventually went. It was the same trip that I was to take. It just seemed like fate had stepped in.

We met in Vancouver. My girlfriend and I had gone from Toronto to Calgary and had an overnight stay, then we took the train. It was during the tour that I turned 56. When we arrived at Vancouver I saw this man at the train station waiting to join up with the tour. I looked at him and thought how very sad he looked. I thought he had a very sad face. It was Bill. During the tour I would see him walking around with the group. On the way back on the deck of the boat, I was sitting by myself looking over the water. My friend was talking to him and I would look over and I kept noticing that he was looking over at me. When we got back to Vancouver, we went on a walking tour around Chinatown and he was beside me. I took my jacket off as I was hot, and he carried it for me. I remember remarking to him when we first met that I thought he was English. He said no, he was from Australia.

Later on in the evening he asked if my friend and I would like to go down to the cocktail lounge where the others were playing cards. I've since found out that he doesn't like playing cards. So my girlfriend and I went. The next day we had a good chance to talk to each other. Bill must have been around 48 then, so I was a fair bit older than him. We always seemed to be together on walks. In the bus we were supposed to change seats so we weren't beside our partners all the time. I didn't normally sit with my girlfriend, so one time I sat beside Bill and we talked, then on the second night my girlfriend said she was going to play cards. I think

I was mean to her because from then on, every night, I wanted to be with Bill. She was hurt and I don't blame her. Bill and I would go to the cocktail lounge and he'd have a lemon squash. He didn't drink alcohol. I said he didn't need to drink just because I was going to have a cocktail.

He told me about his wife on the second or third evening when we were sitting chatting. He just seemed to unburden himself. I understood how much her death had upset him. They had been married for 20 years and his bereavement was very recent. It was only four months, whereas mine was five years. I knew how I felt by that time because I had gone through the grieving process and I knew if I had a chance to be married again, to the right man, I would. He knew how old I was and I knew how old he was. I was not going to lie about it like some women do. I thought though there was no good me getting serious about this man because he was younger than me. He lived in Australia and probably he just wanted someone to talk to on the tour. I have always been a good listener. I didn't offer any advice; I was just listening.

We only saw each other for seven or eight days and he was leaving the tour after that to go up north. He had added on to his tour to see some cousins on his mother's side whom he had never met. He had their address and he had told them he would go for one or two nights. He was going to be in Toronto from the Sunday to the Wednesday and then he was going to take a side trip to Niagara Falls. He said, 'Is there any chance I can see you when I am in Toronto?' I said that would be wonderful. I was still on holiday and I said I would pick him up at the airport and take him to his hotel. I could tell how he was feeling and how I was feeling. I know he had not forgotten his wife, but his face wasn't quite as sad by now.

There was room on the bus for me to go to Niagara Falls so I spent the day with him. He had met my daughter, as I had him back to our place that first night for dinner. My daughter had the dinner ready for us. She was about 18. Then Bill went off to Montreal and when he came back he had to change planes at Toronto and he phoned me from the airport. He asked if there would be any chance of me and my daughter going to Hawaii, sort of halfway, for a holiday. I said that I would have to think about it. I had used what money I had available for the trip to Vancouver so it meant I would have to sell some of the bonds Frank had bought.

When Bill got back to Sydney, he telephoned and we talked and talked. Then he wrote me a letter asking if there would be any chance that I could get to Australia. He wrote that he could show me around and that he had a house with enough room for me to stay. I didn't think abut it for too long. I went to the bank and they said they would give me a loan, so I didn't have to sell the bonds. I knew how I felt by then. I told my son. He hadn't met Bill, unfortunately. That was partly my fault. I think he wasn't against it, he is very liberal that way, he left the decision up to me. Of course, I wasn't a teenager: I'd been through a marriage. My brother said, 'How do you know what it's going to be like when you are there? Maybe he thinks you have money and he might be a wife beater.' I said I didn't even know if I was marrying him yet.

That was December 1977. My daughter and I made the trip. We stayed for three weeks. I got extra time off because I'd worked overtime. They were very good at work. They all had twinkles in their eyes as though they saw what was coming. The first night after we arrived, Bill drove us to his house and we settled in. It was getting late but he said,

'Look, come on, I've got something to show you in the garage. That was when he proposed to me. Right there in the garage. I had met his two stepsons and their families, they were all there. They were all just so wonderful. I said I would have to think about it. A couple of seconds after I had thought about it I said yes. I knew how I felt. I thought gee, at my age I was not going to meet someone else like this. Yet I hadn't really met all his family. I still had to meet his wife's sister and his brother and sister and all their families.

Bill wanted me to live in Australia rather than him live in Canada because he didn't want to give up his job and his superannuation. My daughter was going to come and live with us so I didn't see any problem there. I hated to leave my brother, who was twelve years older than me, and my sister, who was then living in Mexico. As it turned out, my daughter had been so unhappy in her last year of high school, I said she could leave. She finished in June and went on to business college. Bill and I got married in July in Toronto in 1978. I wanted my son to give me away and my friends were there and my brother was best man.

I thought the age difference—Bill being thirteen years younger—was to my advantage. Although I loved Frank and we had a happy marriage, I felt that I had grown older before my time. Most of my girlfriends had married fellows that were at the same high school or around their age. I hate to say it, but after the heart attack Frank just didn't have the energy to go out that much. He would try to do it for me, but I couldn't expect him to. He would always tell me to go but I hated going out on my own. When I knew that Bill was younger and that he was wanting to marry me, I couldn't believe it. I didn't make any conditions. It just happened that way.

When I went out to Australia I met his family, especially his late wife's family, and they accepted me, even his stepsons. This is what I told my brother when I went back home: everyone has accepted me. I was going to the other end of the earth as far as my brother was concerned. I couldn't have been happier, I don't think I could have married anybody else. My daughter got along well with the younger stepson and his family, but she began to get unhappy and was getting very homesick because she couldn't get a job in Australia. She was fine in Sydney but when we moved to Perth she couldn't get anything. She did what she could. She worked in the petrol station which at one time we owned and ran. She missed her brother, the snow and the skiing and her friends. I said she should go back for Christmas which she did the next year. I had always told her that if she wanted to go back for a holiday that I would pay for it. While she was in Canada, for three months, she got a part-time job at York University, were I had worked. She came back to Perth and apologised, saying she was going to pack up and go back to Toronto. She lived with her brother for a while then she got herself a flat and she met the man she married.

This is going to sound very syrupy but I think it's the kind of man that Bill is that has sustained us, both being in second marriages. I could never think of not being with him. I think that my being able to go back to see my family is so very important. This was one of the things Bill said when we married: if ever I wanted to go back to see my family he would never stop me. I think certain people felt I should have used my mortgage money for our marriage, to buy a house. Once Bill sold his house in Sydney and we moved to Perth, we were just renting. It wasn't good. Every time we'd move, the rent would go up. Finally we decided it couldn't go on. As it happened, the work that Bill was doing just before he retired at 65 was for a retirement hostel in Perth. They thought he was so good at his job they told him he could work until he was 70. He was on call 24 hours a day. If anybody needed help in the middle of the night he was always there. They just didn't want him to leave, but we had this chance of going into a retirement village in Tasmania at a rent we could afford.

We live strictly on a pension—my pension from Canada, and Bill's and my combined pension. I became an Australian citizen on Australia Day. I'm very proud to say so. The place we live in is very small but we are quite comfortable. I suppose it just seems as though we always have something going for us at the last minute. I'm not a very religious person, but I do read a little book called the *Daily Word*. It comes out once a month and there is one day of the month that is called Let go let God. It was my niece over in California, my sister's daughter, who told me about this. She said that whenever I feel that I just can't do anything about a certain situation, I think well, alright, it's in God's hands and that's how I've been feeling since she told me about it. I've been subscribing to it for about six or seven years now. It certainly has helped me to sustain our marriage. Bill is a Presbyterian, but he doesn't feel he needs to go to church. I haven't been going to church but I read my book every day. Since Bill retired, we spend a lot of our time together, although not as much as I would like to. I guess I would say that if there was a downside to the relationship it would be that we don't have as much in common as some people. Our interests aren't as close as some people. Bill doesn't like playing cards. He doesn't like joining clubs. We do find ourselves following the same path, though. This is how I know I feel. I think to myself, I'm 75 and I want to enjoy every day as much as possible with Bill because that's what I married him for—to be with him. When I knew he was retiring I thought, oh, wonderful! Tasmania has a similar climate to Canada so I like it here. The only thing I do notice—and I noticed the same thing in Perth—is that there is no central heating. We have reverse-cycle air conditioning but with no basements, as in Canada, you don't have a furnace and I do feel colder inside the house. I dress warmly to go outside but in the house I always have to have something warm on as well. The loungeroom is heated but the bedroom and bathroom are cold. I suppose I have got used to it.

Bill and I at first found it hard to talk to one another about our previous spouses. I would feel that I didn't want to hear that much about her after we were married but I don't think Bill was like that. I am over that now and I will make reference to her. Sometimes Bill would forget, when we were first married, and tell me what wonderful scones she made and the first and only scones I made were like rocks. I got mad, but I got over that. This was the first year of our marriage. When the person you were married to for 27 years dies and then you remarry and that continues for 20 years, there must be something in that second marriage that is as positive as the first and that keeps you going. The main thing, and I said it before, is the love and respect for each other. This is how I felt with Frank. I admired him so much and he was so tolerant with me. We lived for six years with my parents and he had to put up with a lot. They were wonderful parents, but I was still their little girl. I was the second family in a way. My sister is ten years older and my brother twelve.

Any woman who gets to her mid-fifties, the age that I was when I met Bill, should not give up hope of ever finding someone. They should not just go and marry anybody, of course. Bill wasn't a rich man. He was comfortable and he had a job. To me he was very good looking. My first husband was not what you would call a handsome man, but to me he had the most wonderful eyes. I always look at a person's eyes. The same with Bill. I feel you can tell what sort of person someone is by looking at their eyes.

After President Kennedy was assassinated, I read that his widow Jackie said you don't realise how alone you are until you close the bedroom door. That was just how I felt after Frank died. Not that I needed sex. It's more about having somebody you can talk to. Somebody who cares. That's why you can't just marry anybody. Frank and I had a lot in common. We liked cards, classical music and reading. I like reading novels. Bill doesn't play cards. He likes reading but reads technical books. I like to listen to the symphony. Bill couldn't care less. He likes good music but not classical. If I were to describe what keeps a second marriage going when two people have lost their first partners, I would have to keep getting back to knowing that he cares for me. We had a near-fatal accident with our truck in Perth and I guess we both realised then that life is pretty short. As I said earlier, I could not be happier. I could not have married anybody else and I still think that, after almost twenty years. I was very lucky.

ROSEMARY

Rosemary and Mike lived together for a number of years before they married. It was a second marriage for Mike, the first for Rosemary. After a less than harmonious time together, Rosemary fled the matrimonial home, returning to complete the business of burying her husband only two years later. We spoke about the dilemma she faced in being asked to take care of the funeral arrangements for her husband, along with the strong bond she built with her stepdaughter during the ensuing years. She also spoke of the need to develop her own business and personal interests after the tragedy of a separation and ultimately, the death of her husband.

Mike and I were married for seven and a half years. He died of a weakness in his heart known as Marfan's syndrome. He hadn't known that he had the disease. At the time he died he had been swimming—in a public swimming pool—and he simply collapsed. At least I think he collapsed; I wasn't there. We had in fact been separated for four years. I had moved from the city in which we lived and away from the marital home.

We had both worked full-time while we were married. Mike was a senior public servant and I was on the personal staff of a Member of Parliament, a minister. I was 26 when we first got together and 30 when we were married. Mike was fourteen years older than me and he had been married before. He had two daughters by his previous marriage. He was married for around fourteen years before he met and married me.

He died in 1987. I left him in 1983 and moved north. I had an apartment lined up and I had removalists come in and pick up half the furniture. I hid for a night at a friend's place around the corner from where we had lived so that he couldn't come and find me. I stayed with a girlfriend who had been very understanding. She was a great help but I don't think a network of friends, especially women friends, is a conscious thing—they just exist. She was happy to have me stay the night. Friends also change over the years. Sometimes friends are not there for a good many years of your life at times, through a certain period—because of where you may be living, for example. That woman, the person who was close to me then, I haven't seen for years. It could be said—and it certainly was said by Mike at the time—that she influenced me, influenced my decision to leave him. But that wasn't the case.

He wasn't very happy about me leaving—naturally, I suppose, because he didn't know it was going to happen. Throughout the time that we were together he would just up and disappear. Sometimes he would be fine for a couple of months or so, then he'd just get very strange and disappear. Sometimes he'd be out for a night and I'd find the car and he was off somewhere drinking. Sometimes he'd disappear for three or four days. He'd always go to work and then he'd just come back. And I'd be there. Then finally he said he'd taken a lease on an apartment because he wanted some space so I suggested that if he'd taken a lease on an apartment perhaps he should take a whole lot more space, than he was intending and move into it. I'd had enough. I said if he had taken a lease he could go and live in it permanently, which was a bit of a surprise—a surprise to me, because I didn't think I'd say something like that. Then he moved out, sort of, so I said that was enough. I moved out and he went back to the house. I made up a list of the furniture.

I wouldn't tell him where I had moved to for a while and then I had contact with his daughter, Sarah. She was living with us when I left. She was my stepdaughter and I had a good relationship with her. Sarah came to live with us when she was about 14 or 15 so she was with us—well, me—for some years. He kept disappearing. I moved north and got a job and didn't have any contact with him for a while then, gradually, there was contact. If he came up here I would see him and he would want me to go back—even though there was another woman. When I left, she was a bit closer to him than I wanted—she actually moved in with him a few months after I left. That was the time he pleaded with me to go back. I said it was a touch crowded down there at the moment. Interestingly, that relationship didn't work in the sense of her living there so she moved out. I think the last time I spoke to him was about three or four weeks before he died. He'd just ring and want to talk.

He collapsed in the swimming pool and they got a helicopter to take him to hospital, but he died on the way. Sarah rang me some time in the afternoon. It was Sunday. I just asked her where we went from there because, when somebody dies, you don't know what your first move should be. It didn't occur to me, in the beginning, to say well, where's the body? Where is he? I thought for a while then decided I'd better find out where he was. It turned out he was still at the hospital. It was not that easy to find out. We don't think about those things. I suppose we expect that we will die when we are with family or friends and that it will all work out nicely. It's not always that simple and I get a little bit angry with funeral directors because they come in and they're all terribly nice but they don't tell you how much anything costs. Here you are with all sorts of things to work out—not least your grief and anguish—and they start you off at the expensive end. Sarah said it was about $7000 for the funeral. It's almost as if they're trading on the fact that you are all in shock and you don't know what to do. It seems a bit harsh to say that in retrospect, but I think they have a duty to say, well OK, we are actually selling things and this is what it is going to cost.

There was a procession of people going into the funeral service, looking shocked. The two girlfriends were interesting. It transpired that Mike was going out with a number of ladies at the same time and had been for a number of years. I actually found this quite funny. They only found out about each other and their relationships with Mike in the dining room of the house after the funeral. They both went to see Sarah after the funeral. I sat in the other room. It's amazing what people leave behind. I suppose truth is what you want to believe. I certainly don't believe they had their eyes open when they went into relationships with him. Anyway, we got the funeral director sorted out, Sarah and I, and then we had to get Mike buried. The next thing is, what do you do with him? The funeral director took the body but Mike always said he didn't want to be cremated. He used to get really upset because we would say, 'We're gonna burn you when you die.' I don't know why he would get upset but we had to face that. It is funny really. We laughed about it then, when we were poking fun at him, but when he was dead it really began to matter because what he wanted in life became a reality. You've got to respect people's wishes. Because he was born a Catholic and his mother was coming over, we gave him a Catholic funeral which was very interesting. His first wife wasn't a Catholic and I wasn't either. Neither was he, really. I don't think his daughters were even baptised. But we did it for his mother anyway. I didn't spend much time in town. Only a couple of nights and then back for the funeral a week later. Having girlfriends at the funeral was like something out of a television soap opera. It was just very difficult. Can you imagine the scene? There am I with his mother, whom I have never met, who flew out from Scotland for the funeral. I picked her up at the airport. I had said that if anyone wanted me to come down, I'd come down, but I wasn't sure it was appropriate for me to be there. I said I would do whatever Sarah wanted me to do. They—that is, his mother and Sarah—decided they wanted me to be there, so I went down. His first wife was living in Hong Kong with his other daughter, but only the daughter came over for the funeral. His first wife did say, on the telephone, something like, 'Thank you for being there for the girls,' but I was a bit angry about that because I thought she had a duty to them and to him. Anyway, I was there.

The funeral service was interesting. I'd only ever been to one funeral and I didn't quite know what to do. It was all full-on with incense being thrown all over the coffin. Mike's mother said, God, he won't like that very much. Then there were the two girlfriends sitting in the back, in the stalls. Lots of tears. From them. I didn't cry. If I had still been with him it would have been different, but to me it was just a sad occasion. I didn't go and see the body before the funeral but I should have. I know now how important that is. I think it closes the door. You have to acknowledge death in some formal sense. For a long time I regretted not seeing him. I think I've almost got over it now, nearly ten years later.

By this stage I had started my own business. In fact, I had started it about two years before he died. I had a year before that working with a large theatrical management agency and during that time I decided I was unemployable. I just wouldn't take orders. Previously I'd been in a job where I had been left to my own devices pretty much, with the government minister. I had developed a lot in the sense of what I knew and what I was able to do and then suddenly I was in a job where, while I was told 'We will make you fly and you'll have a fantastic time', all the managing director wanted was somebody to order around. It was funny because he had come looking for me in the first place. He knew the minister and he knew that, when the government changed, some of us were on the market. I said no the first time. I just didn't know what I wanted to do and he wouldn't offer me enough money, which he later increased. That was in 1984.

At the end of that I had a little bit of money so I thought I'd see what I could do for myself. I thought I would set up a business running social functions for business people. I'm good at organising. I'm good at dealing with people. So I got myself all set up—put a desk in the second bedroom, bought a trading name, sent out three thousand fliers to post office boxes and sat at home waiting for somebody to call. But they didn't. I tried it for a couple of months and didn't sort of do anything. My problem was I didn't know which way to go. I also had a talk to somebody who was running a big travel group who told me that I'd never be a leader and I'd never make it in my own business because I needed somebody to direct all the time. He didn't need to tell me something like that. It was a bit of a red rag to a bull.

I went home to England for a couple of months, later that year, and sat around wondering what to do with myself. This was in 1985. I did actually get a couple of small jobs before that, organising conferences, and I organised a Christmas party for a computer company so I had started to get my foot in the door. I came back because a girlfriend said she had tickets to go and see some show, or something. I was sitting around feeling sorry for myself and she wrote and said I should come back because she had these tickets, so I packed up and came back. Can you believe that? Halfway around the world for a show. I suppose I was really getting restless anyway and needed to return. Once I arrived, I did a bit of temporary work and gradually got some other work, a few hours here and there, and I got a few more contacts which helped. Then another friend asked me to help her put some conferences together and that was what really got me into what I am doing now, in the conference industry. I started writing conference programs for a national financial newspaper and I eventually was doing enough work for them so I could stop doing all the other smaller jobs.

Business became a pretty strong focus in my life at this stage. It steadily grew over the first five years and it was only when it started to grow a bit too fast that I lost the plot. At that early stage, I kept Mike at a distance because I knew how strong a pull he had on me. I deliberately wouldn't see him for the first twelve months and on the rare occasion that I did he was wanting me to go back. He was always on the telephone wanting me to go back and, to be honest, if he hadn't died I'm not sure I wouldn't have gone back to him. That's something I'll never know but that's how strong it was. If he were still alive he'd be 61. He always regarded me as being strong enough to do what I wanted to do and he would never interfere with what I was doing in a work sense. So I suppose by now he may have been supportive and non-controlling. There are passages of time when someone is closer to you but for one reason or another they move on, or you move away, or they get too controlling and you want them to go away which is what happened with one girlfriend—the one whose house I stayed in when I moved away. She wanted to take over my life and I wasn't particularly pleased about that.

When Mike died, I was actually living with another man. It had been two years since I had left Mike. I don't think my involvement with his burial affected that relationship. I was with that man for eight years. Even then, Sarah was always part of my life. She had always been there. She has now been living with me again for the past two years. Prior to that, even when I was in that other relationship—which has now dissolved—she would come and stay. She might stay a week or more. Or at one stage, when she herself had a heart operation, she came and stayed with me for a long period, a couple of months or more. She always seemed to be around whenever I moved house. Sarah is family. Family but not quite. More of a friend. Depends whether she's doing something I don't like, even though she's 32 and I'm 47.

She has the same thing Mike had—Marfan's syndrome—and she's got to be on drugs for the rest of her life and undergo tests every month. She's also got to go back into hospital and have another operation. You don't fix Marfan's syndrome, all you can do is watch it. It's about four years since she had the first operation. She was in Hong Kong at the time and was sick with something else when they discovered she also had Marfan's sydnrome. Her mother rang me to tell me and Sarah decided she wanted to be operated on here rather than in Hong Kong so she moved in with me. She went back and forward to Hong Kong for a year or so after the operation but decided to come back here permanently if she could get a job, which she did. By that stage I had moved out of the relationship I was in, so I said if she could get a job she could move in with me permanently. She thought it was a great idea.

We always got on well. We have been quite close because the four of us would always go away for Christmas holidays when the girls were younger. I think they approved of Mike's choice when he married me. And they supported it even though he didn't tell them for about a year, officially, that he was living with me before we got married. They remember the first time they saw me because I had long hair and my fingernails were painted and I kept running them through my hair. They always remember that.

I think I was fortunate when I moved away. I moved into a two-storey terrace which was divided into two apartments and there was a woman upstairs who had recently moved out from her guy so we got to know each other. She had a network of friends and that network was a very welcome one. It was a network of people who didn't have close family ties so it just developed over the years. It is fortunate that people I know now are not people I have met at work. I wasn't reliant on my work to have a social life. It's important to keep the two separate, especially when you are a single woman working for yourself. I think people gravitate towards or relate to people who are in similar circumstances. Most of my friends at that time, most of the people I was with and have stayed friends with, are single— male or female. None had family here. Some were English. I'd never known as many English people in my life as I knew here. I don't feel comfortable with people with young families because that's a group that works in isolation to a certain extent. They have their own set of priorities that you can't really fit in with. Other groups, such as divorcees, have their own networks, of necessity. One girlfriend who's in that category would say the same thing. She has her own friends from university, friends she met when she was single and working and then she's got others who are single mothers like herself because there's a need to have that support group. That's the group that I know. We are all independently minded—not always during our lives, I suppose, but we are pretty strong.

I have never wanted children of my own. I made that decision when I was 32. It was a conscious decision and I had my tubes tied. I think it had something to do with the situation I was in—I was still with Mike, a couple of times I thought I was pregnant and I just didn't want to be because I didn't want to be stuck there with a kid. At that stage I didn't know where Mike was most of the time, sleeping in fields or out with other women. But also I never had any feeling that I would like to be a mother. There was not even a little biological desire to have a baby. My relationship with Sarah is different. That is something which has just evolved. She is a very open person, so it goes both ways. Both of Mike's girls were very open and receptive towards me being in their lives. I don't ever remember having difficulty with them on anything. I never tried to stand between their father and them, or their natural mother. I think we developed a trust, and there is a bond especially with Sarah. Even if Mike had still been alive, my relationship with Sarah would have been good. When Sarah had her heart operation, her mother came over from Hong Kong with her and it was the first time I had met her. She said to me, 'I've told the specialist that Sarah has got two mothers.' Sarah is a director of my company now. She probably looks after me more than I look after her.

It takes a long time coming to terms with the fact that somebody you were very close to doesn't exist any more—at least, exist in the sense that you knew them. Even if you were washed up with them, or you think you were, you just never really accept that they are not there. I don't know why. You just don't. Maybe because it's so sudden. Gone. Maybe there's a difference between somebody who dies suddenly and somebody who lingers for a while. In that situation it's inevitable and you are working towards an end. You know it's going to come to an end within a time frame, but when somebody you spoke to just before is not there, there are all these things that are unfinished. I don't think you can spend your life thinking about what you should do in a relationship in case that happens. After all, we are only human beings. I don't think we ever think of death as getting in the way of things. You can't live your life thinking, 'I need to live my life in a particular way with this person because they might die tomorrow.' What sort of mistakes might you make in that? You would be handcuffing yourself to something you could not deal with. You just have to do the best you can. Don't live as if tomorrow's going to be the finish.

I don't know if it's because I had left Mike before he died or not, but I think I would marry again, as opposed to living with someone. I don't think I would get together with someone for the sake of convenience, though. I would marry again if the emotion was right—if the feeling was there. Not just trust. I can't really explain it, it's an emotional thing. I wanted to marry Mike, but I didn't want to marry the guy I was with after Mike. I could never have married him, even though we were together for eight years—despite the fact he would ask once a year.

I go to the gym a lot now. What I do outside work, though, doesn't form itself into categories. I enjoy my work. I've never really had sporting interests. I've never been particularly interested in football and that sort of thing. I don't think a long way ahead in life. I basically work on the assumption that I can do anything I want to do if I put my mind to it. I have to survive on my own because I don't seem to be capable of surviving with someone else, so anything I do is a cushion for me in the future and I'm trying to be careful not to get distracted and to be a cushion for someone else. I don't want to do dual support. If I'm going to support anybody, it will be me, and whoever I tie up with again—and I'm sure I will—they will have to be able to support themselves in a whole lot of ways, not just monetarily.

On the other hand I don't have any idea of where I will be in ten or twenty years' time. In the past 25 years, whichever direction I took I didn't think that was going to be the direction I would take and I would wonder how I ended up there. I don't have the capacity to plan ahead. I should have. It concerns me that I don't. Because other people seem to know. On the other hand, I know I am resourceful and I am a survivor and one way or the other I'll get through whatever it is I'm faced with. I would like to think I am not going to be on my own. But then I don't want to be with someone who is a burden. And I don't want to be with someone who is controlling because I wouldn't be very nice to live with. I don't like being controlled. You don't get to 47 and not be able to make some of your own decisions. You don't need someone who is controlling. On the other hand, I don't have a need to be in control; it is just a need to have the respect from someone else so that I am able to make my own decisions. I am a pretty adaptable soul. I'm pretty easy to get on with, I would say. Others may not. In terms of a constant in my life, my strength comes from my family—from my parents, who have always been there in a very non-judgemental sense to say, 'Well we knew if you went down that road it might not work, but we did not want to tell you that because you had to work it out for yourself.' I also have an older brother living in Canada and, even though I don't see him much, I know he is there and that is still a support in a way.

I am also involved in Rotary these days. I was invited by a girlfriend, for business and personal reasons, and I have been involved with it now for more than a year. I enjoy it in a sense that it's another dimension to my life. It's not a substitute for one thing or another. It's not where I seek my social life—there's work, there's Rotary and there's the social thing. The line between Rotary and social is a bit overlapping because of some of the people who are in Rotary. I enjoy it because most of the people in it are like me and I am doing something. Something worthwhile comes out of it. It achieves something that I can't achieve in other business or social arrangements.

I don't think I would go out and start a new business venture at this time of my life. Not something entirely new. I wouldn't know what to do. I wouldn't leave what I have got. What I have got now is an investment in my future. What I am thinking now is that I am 47, so I've probably got ten years of really effective, valuable time—which doesn't mean I can't work—ten years to make the most of everything. There are lots of younger people coming through who have better selling abilities than I have and there's the whole thing of recognising that I am working in a very competitive industry so I have to stay near the front, I have to make it work and I have to make it valuable. I can't just make it a wage. When I turn 55 I'll put someone out in front who is about 40.

After that, well Sarah has already said she will look after me when I am an old lady, when I am a cripple. She'll wheel me down the stairs. The same way I would look after her. Even though she likes dreadful music. I often think about our relationship. While it is a family thing, it is a family thing that I am not forced into. With families, whatever happens you have to acknowledge the fact that they exist. With Sarah, we could have just gone our separate ways, so there is a bond there that is probably from affection and that probably evolved from the whole time I was with Mike, but we also quite like each other and we don't get in each other's way.

Still, if I said don't do something, like a mother, she wouldn't do it. And if she said to me don't do that, I wouldn't. But she wouldn't say that sort of thing. She doesn't ring in, or things like that, if she's away but she doesn't do it because the relationship she has had with her mother has never been to report in. Her mother will come over here for two weeks and she might see Sarah for half a day. They're still close, but there has never been that reporting thing.

It was a difficult decision to leave Mike. I think I did it for my own survival, rather than his. I don't know if I wanted to go, but I had to. Mind you, you wonder how much your job keeps your mind off your problems because, when I was working for the government minister, I had the opportunity to travel so when there was something happening at home I could disappear for a few days or whatever. When that job changed, I didn't work for a couple of months and then I went to an entirely different sort of job where I didn't get out of the office. So while all that rubbish was going on, that's all I had to concentrate on. Maybe the other job kept my mind off it. I don't think people should do things to take their minds off something else. I think they have to have a balance in their lives that allows them to cope with the ups and downs of work and the personal side of life. Too many people just rely on the other person in their life and that's not good. I think it's important when two people decide to be together that they are almost part of each other. But it's equally important that they must be independent of each other. They don't have to go out and do things separately. They just have to be independent. I think it's entirely possible to achieve both.

Postscript: Late last year Rosemary's stepdaughter Sarah succumbed to the disease which claimed her father's life. She was 33. She had been living with Rosemary for a number of years and their bond was greater than simply stepmother and stepdaughter. They were, Rosemary says, best friends. Sarah died after a regular workout at a gym. She collapsed and was taken to hospital. At her funeral, her friends talked of her life, played the music she loved and spent time contemplating the reality of death. Afterwards, they, along with Sarah's mother who had travelled from Hong Kong, went back to Rosemary's. Sarah's things were still there. Everyone cried.

BONDS OF CIRCUMSTANCE

If there is a central theme to the stories you have just read, it is that widowhood is unlike many other human situations. It is a state most women never plan for, especially young women.

We all live with the knowledge that death is inevitable, but we trust—if we think about it at all—that it will come to us in old age or when we are asleep. We don't plan to be widowed, or widowered, and to spend the remainder of our lives without our husbands or wives. So when it happens—whether suddenly or after a period of illness—we suffer a variety of emotions.

This book shows how some women have coped with the massive trauma of the death of a partner and its associated grief and despair, but it also provides some insights about how to keep personal, business and family affairs in order after the event. It reveals the feelings of sadness and loss we experience but don't necessarily share until someone asks us to. It is about the bonds of circumstance that emerge when we discover others in a similar position. And it is about the universality of widowhood.

Some of the women with whom I spoke while working on this book are not included for reasons of space, but their stories stay in my mind. Sadie had twelve months to prepare for the death of her husband, Stuart, but when he died she still felt disoriented:

'It was a lovely June afternoon. As I waited for a taxi home I had the strangest experience. I thought "I'm a widow". I'd never thought I would be a widow and I was looking at it in a detached sort of way, thinking "This is extraordinary". I had to get back to look after the cats and that was the saving grace—to have something or someone to look after, to think about beside yourself. That was terribly important. You can't sit down grieving and wringing your hands and carrying on. I had done my grieving earlier, privately, and I knew that it was inevitable.'

For another older woman, Lyn, the finality of the loss of her husband Doug meant there were certain things she could never do again because of the shock of the moment:

'I had been with Doug in the hospital a short time before he died, but had then come home. I stayed at home so that the hospital could get me right away if it became necessary. It was in the middle of the day. I was eating a pear when they rang me, and I've never eaten a pear since.'

Widowhood is not restricted to urban women, nor to those who spend their lives outside large cities, although due simply to the demographics of the modern world, the former may be more common. On the surface, there may appear to be more structural support available in urban areas, however, the reality is often very different. These stories show that support sometimes comes from unexpected sources, but at other times has to be actively sought.

Widowhood is not solely the province of the old. Some of the women in this book express concern that structural or institutional support is restricted to the aged, but witness then those older women who have found little in the way of support available to them. Younger women often have young children to care and provide for and, as the stories of Jenny and Hisako show, this can be both a burden and a blessing in managing day-to-day life. Older women do not always have the option of work available to them and this may cause extra financial worry as well.

It is important to consider how you pursue existing relationships: what can be expected; what has changed; what will the nature of those relationships be in the future? How friends and relatives deal with death is critical to how you see yourself in the world after your partner's loss. The continuation and support of existing family, friend and workplace relationships can have a direct bearing on how quickly you feel able to return to day-to-day activities.

For many, the death of a partner reveals the true nature of friendship. It is not always those who are first off the mark with condolences who are still around months later. Some new widows, like Annabelle, experience the unpleasantness of acquaintances who offer to do 'deals', arrange finances, assist with investment, when the real nature of their friendship is self-interest. Others, Helen for example, discover that there are friends in unusual places, friends who are willing to take a great deal of time to assist in the healing process. There are those like Michele who gain great support from unusual quarters: the people who worked with her husband and her own ex-employer who, although under no moral or legal obligation to provide financial support, yet took it upon himself and his family to do so.

Widowhood brings strange and unknown circumstances. We all have a social responsibility to embrace people in this situation and make them feel they are not outcasts, yet it is generally others in similar circumstances who respond most readily. In the modern world of insularity and cultural fragmentation—in which there is a failure to understand the need for displays of public emotion—there is a tendency to forget that there are those who need our emotional support.

Why are we unable to deal with death on a personal and intimate level? Death, however unfortunate, is a very real part of life, and we can make the lives of those dealing with the reality much easier by acknowledging their grief and supporting them as they make choices and decisions about their changed world.

Since I completed work on this book, the snowball effect has continued. I find myself talking with a group of people and the publication of the book may come up in conversation. Many women have then revealed their status as widows, whereas in general conversation they feel they should keep it to themselves, especially when meeting someone for the first time.

This is critically important. It tells us how women, especially younger women, feel about their status as 'a widow'. Most of them—including a woman senior police constable I met at a barbecue—believe they are put in an awkward social position if they reveal their widowhood. But this should never be an embarrassing or confrontational situation. Indeed, it is the inability of others to deal with the realities of your loss that may then lead to acute or uncomfortable silences, followed by a need to top up drinks, check in the kitchen, or find some other way to physically remove themselves from the twofold problem: mortality and someone who might need support and succour.

There is still a great deal for us all to learn about how best to provide support to those who must deal with loss and grief in a modern world where we are increasingly distanced from the reality of death. The gap between widows and others in the community needs to be bridged, with society acknowledging that widows and widowers need and deserve far more than they get in terms of support and assistance— moral, financial and social.

I hope the stories in this book assist in this process.

To those of you who now face life as a widow, don't be embarrassed or feel awkward or shy about your situation. Make your needs for support and reassurance known to others—people are often very pleased to be asked for help even though they may not know how to offer. Your experience is unique, but you are not alone.